118.

Throw Away the Medicine Bottle

And Replace it with a Jar of

This is the Jar, and
It's Full to the Top.

VEGEMITE

THE WONDERFUL

VITAMIN FOOD

VEGEMITE

Deficiency of Vitamin in our food
is the chief cause of stomachic troubles
and nervous disorders.

VEGEMITE taken at every meal re-
charges your food with VITAMIN and
puts you on the road to lasting good
health.

National Library of Australia

THE MAN WHO INVENTED VEGEMITE

Jamie Callister has worked in television media, advertising and the building industries. The grandson of Cyril Callister, this is his first book. Jamie lives on the south Queensland coast with his wife and three children.

Rod Howard is a journalist and author of numerous books. *The Fabulist: The Incredible Story of Louis De Rougemont* is currently in development as a feature film and *A Forger's Tale: The Extraordinary Story of Henry Savery* was the 2011 winner of the FAW Walter Stone Award for biography. Rod lives in Bellingen, New South Wales, with his wife and two sons.

THE MAN WHO INVENTED

Vegemite

The true story behind
an Australian icon

JAMIE CALLISTER
with
ROD HOWARD

Published in Australia in 2011 by Pier 9, an imprint of Murdoch Books Pty Limited

Murdoch Books Australia
Pier 8/9
23 Hickson Road
Millers Point NSW 2000
Phone: +61 (0) 2 8220 2000
Fax: +61 (0) 2 8220 2558
www.murdochbooks.com.au
info@murdochbooks.com.au

Murdoch Books UK Limited
Erico House, 6th Floor
93–99 Upper Richmond Road
Putney, London SW15 2TG
Phone: +44 (0) 20 8785 5995
Fax: +44 (0) 20 8785 5985
www.murdochbooks.co.uk
info@murdochbooks.co.uk

Text © Jamie Callister 2012
The moral right of the author has been asserted.
Cover design by Lanz+Martin
Text design by Robert Polmear
Index by John M. Peter

A cataloguing-in-publication entry is available from the catalogue of the National Library of Australia at www.nla.gov.au.

ISBN 9781742668567

Printed in Australia by Griffin Press

The paper this book is printed on is certified against the Forest Stewardship Council® Standards. Griffin Press holds FSC chain of custody certification SGS-COC-005088. FSC promotes environmentally responsible, socially beneficial and economically viable management of the world's forests.

In memory of my uncle
Flight Sergeant Ian Hope Callister
79 Squadron RAAF

Contents

Prologue

I loved the fish that used to hang on the wall of my father's study. It wasn't just any fish: it was a perfectly preserved fossil, a broad black outline against a soft-coloured flat stone about the size of a trout, only with a prehistoric head. When I was a child, I would climb up on the low bookshelf next to the television and, with one foot on the cabinet, triumphantly unhook the wire holding the fish to the wall. I'd then sit on the couch admiring my catch. It was heavy and cold to touch and I was never disappointed by it, though it smelled of dust or rock – definitely not fish.

After a while I would then turn my attention to the photos, paintings and scrolls on the wall, trying to work out who the people in them were and what they meant. My older brother and I shared a bedroom, which at age seven I loved but at seventeen he hated. Our maternal Nan had come to live with us because it was 'our turn'. Cupboards had been cleared out and the junk all ended up in our room. We searched through it, eyes wide.

We found World War II flying gloves, a kit bag, a flight logbook and, at the bottom of one of the boxes, two brown folders containing countless letters and newspaper clippings. We pored over them, fascinated. I couldn't read the letters very well but I loved the emblems at the top of each page. I became custodian of the folders and my brother took the logbook.

One day he took me into our father's study and explained what it all meant. The man in the photo immediately to the right of the fossilised fish was my Uncle Ian – Dad's brother – aged about nineteen. Below and above him were two watercolours of single-seater fighter planes in mid-flight. One was a Spitfire, the other a Hurricane. My brother said the Spitfire was Uncle Ian's plane. Nearly half a century later I know it wasn't. The man in the photo next to the painting of the Spitfire was my grandfather. He had meticulously filed every letter his son had written to him while he was away at the war. In the photo, somebody had loosely draped their arm over my grandfather's shoulders, but nobody in the family knew whose arm it was. Concluding the 'rogues' gallery', as Mum often called it, was a big scroll which read, 'Cyril Percy Callister, Doctor of Science'. Back then I remember it sounded very grand, though my immediate reaction was to thank God I wasn't called Cyril (or Percy for that matter).

Dad always referred to my grandfather as 'the old man'. I never met him. I knew that he had been a chemist or scientist and had spent most of his working life at the big food company Kraft. I vividly remember one morning when I was still very young, the whole family sitting down to breakfast. Dad had lathered his toast with Vegemite and announced, with a great flourish, 'You either love it or hate it. But you should never forget that the old man invented it.'

We looked to Mum for confirmation and she nodded. We were all impressed, though the odd person I told this news to always seemed more interested than me. Later I remember that Dad was sometimes called on to do television interviews on anniversaries of Vegemite or other special occasions. He was clearly proud of his father's achievements.

On occasions we would visit Dad's sister. Jean was a small woman with a stoop and a marked limp. She was the eldest child, followed by Ian and then my father. An identical photo of Ian hung on Auntie Jean's wall, too, and my eldest cousin was named after him. On most visits, Auntie Jean spoke more of her mother than her father. She told stories of travelling overseas as a young girl and of her mother's childhood in Scotland. Dad usually referred to her (as his mother had) as 'wee Bonnie Jean'.

On other occasions I met great uncles and aunts who held me in uncomfortable embraces and couldn't decide who I looked like most – sometimes Dad, sometimes Ian, sometimes even Cyril. As I grew older that extended family, that living connection with the past, slowly shrank.

By the late 1990s, my mother had passed away and my father was getting on. Sorting through his papers one day, he said to me, 'You know, Jic, you can look after any stuff that comes up about the old man. If anyone rings I'll put them through to you.' My main concern was what I would say in reply. He just smiled and said, 'You know the story.'

I wasn't so sure.

I went back to the brown folders and the letters my brother and I had scrutinised as kids. There was one document in particular that had a special resonance. I think it was meant for me. It was not a letter but it was written by my grandfather and it highlighted his intellect, integrity and despair. As I finished reading it to my wife early one summer morning, I looked up and saw her brush away a tear. She whispered, 'Your grandfather died from a broken heart.'

It was the starting point that took me back.

The Age of Discovery

*A*s the young Cyril Callister approached the dinner table his assistant held out a feather in her trembling hand. There was a hush among the audience, for all seven siblings knew this might be the last such performance. The older boys would soon be leaving on an uncertain journey.

It was exciting, if somewhat hazardous, living with a budding scientist. In the early days, before half the brood was even born, it was their father William Callister who had mesmerised the family with his conjuring tricks. The phosphorus that had glowed with a ghoulish green light on his fingertips, the bottles of water that would miraculously change colour. Cyril assisted, watching intently and deducing by careful observation the sorcerer's secrets. Shortly after he completed primary school the mantle was passed to him.

In the ensuing years, the Callister family witnessed many amazing feats and the occasional disaster. On one occasion, Cyril nearly gassed them all while distilling a volatile brew of hydrogen sulphide and ammonia. The resulting rotten egg stench had stunk out the house for days. On another occasion, he combined zinc and hydrochloric acid to produce sufficient hydrogen to elevate a small Indian rubber balloon. But the 'exploding spider' was the firm family favourite.

In the middle of the table, at a safe distance from curious young fingers, stood a wire cake stand. On it rested a thin sheet of paper smeared in a browny black paste. Cyril took the feather from his sister and with a flourish and a twirl moved it towards the stand. When the feather was just about to touch the paper, he hesitated a moment for effect, just like his father before him. As ever, there was a collective gasp.

Then in a flash it was done. The feather had barely brushed the paper when there was a loud bang and a shot of flame, accompanied by a cloudburst of violet smoke. Shrieks of delight erupted around the table. The ammonia and iodine solution had worked its wonders again. William beamed with pride, Cyril gave the feather a final ceremonial flourish and Aunt Eadie shook her head.

My grandfather was born in 1893 at Chute, a remnant Victorian goldfield town about sixty-five kilometres west of Ballarat. These were uncertain times. The gold boom of the previous decades had been followed by the inevitable bust. Property prices plunged, banks collapsed and foreign capital evaporated.

In May 1893, in a drastic attempt to staunch the economic bleeding and arrest the run on funds, the Victorian government declared a five-day bank holiday. Not everyone complied. According to a Reserve Bank publication, the measure helped alleviate the panic, but also drew further attention to those banks that shut their doors.

The region had once yielded immense riches, but the successes of local mining ventures, led by companies with names such as Band of Hope, had long since faded. In the early days, two hundred ounces of gold had been triumphantly excavated from a single claim in just three weeks. Attempts to replicate this bonanza by sinking deeper and deeper shafts met with limited success. Without hope to sustain them, many workers moved on to mine the depths of despair elsewhere. Only the slowly collapsing shafts and mullock heaps dotted throughout the Trawalla Creek valley remained to memorialise their labour.

The Chute school that had once run riot with miners' offspring, and that Cyril's father William had himself attended as a boy, dwindled with the desertion of the claims. William Callister was now the school's only teacher. In the year of Cyril's birth, austerity measures saw his already slight salary cut by a third and the Callister family descend into poverty. Cyril was the third child in a family of nine. One of his siblings, like many in those difficult times, did not survive infancy.

As the smoke from the 'exploding spider' cleared, William clapped his hands and ordered the children to wash up for tea. Cyril and his elder brother Reg let them disperse before cleaning up the dinner table debris.

Cyril was shorter than Reg, four years his junior and wore his thick brown hair parted in the centre. He was a handsome young man with striking pale blue eyes and, when he chose to display it, a slightly crooked grin.

Moving from school to school made making friends hard. The children had even been forced to attend two schools at once, spending three days at one and two at the other to make up numbers. It meant a walk of several kilometres but they were seldom late, even on the days when the creeks were in full flood and they dashed wildly down the banks chasing paper boats.

The Callister family lived at the rear of the schoolhouse, surrounded by abandoned fields known as Trunk Lead. When the children began to outgrow the few rooms, Cyril and Reg were sent to sleep in a draught-ridden loft. Some kilometres away was Carngham Station, near Ballarat, where William agisted cows and horses at the price of his children spending freezing winters repairing fences.

Without a police presence, the local pub was run on nobody's rules and helped keep the district poor. Goldfield prejudices still ran deep and the family often made jokes at the expense of their Catholic neighbours. It was said the Chisholm family couldn't get through a game of football without a fight and the local Irish couldn't play cricket because they lacked self-control whenever the umpire made an unfavourable decision.

All the Callister children had their list of chores, dictated by the necessities of pioneering life: milking, feeding, grooming, washing, darning, ironing, wood chopping, fire lighting and the inevitable washing-up. Baking and bathing were done on Fridays. Hand-me-downs were handed down until there was nothing left but thread, and new clothes were almost unheard of. Cyril's younger sister Florrie received her first new dress at the age of thirteen. William soled and heeled their boots.

The grocer came from Ballarat once a week on Tuesday and mail came three days a week in a 'loose bag' – but only if a minimum number of articles were handled, which meant that the children wrote more letters than they wanted to.

Without refrigeration, food spoilt in summer and worsened in winter. Meat, whether sourced from a lovingly reared animal that had had its throat slit and carcass hung, or bought half-maggoty from a passing cart, barely lasted a week. Most was too tough to eat without being minced for sausages or stewed until all taste was expunged. Canned meat was available but was expensive and either rendered too salty or too bland by the manufacturing processes involved.

Domestic preservation of fruit and vegetables was an ancient but imperfect art that frequently resulted in half the carefully harvested and pickled produce emerging mouldy when lids were lifted. The increasingly large range of products available from the Ballarat grocer was beyond the strictly managed Callister household budget. Luckily the cows gave milk and the hens laid eggs. Breakfast most days was home-baked bread and child-churned butter. No one complained if there was nothing to spread on top.

Apart from the scientific experiments, entertainment was provided by the eldest girl Alice on the school piano. Their mother Rose often sang, though it was confessed long after her premature passing that she may not have had the finest voice in the district. A photo of my great-grandmother captures her tightly corseted figure in regal pose, her hand resting on a gatepost. The only surviving image of my great-grandfather is

9

of him holding a beaker in a laboratory.

As a young man, William's marked intellect and determination set him apart from other goldfields' students. He won a position as a pupil teacher at age fourteen, spent a year at the University of Melbourne and then two years at teacher's college. He told Cyril that he walked almost everywhere, as a tuppence tram fare would have been an extravagance. He sent money home to help with finances, and returned to farm work during the holidays. When he graduated, he commenced teaching in Ballarat. By all accounts he was a strict disciplinarian who believed utterly in the value of hard work.

William could recite the classics and recount tales from history but it was the sciences that captivated him and became his passion. In all his children he fostered a thirst for knowledge. He spoke to them as adults and encouraged them to develop an awareness of the world around them.

William could often be found in the laboratory at the Ballarat School of Mines, carefully measuring substances and using the most modern technical equipment. Later, Cyril would join him. From an early age William's young apprentice had a sound grasp of chemistry and enjoyed exploring the ways various elements reacted with one another. There were spectacular mishaps and near disasters, but Cyril was so keen that his father often had to drag him away to make the trip home before nightfall. It soon became plain that my grandfather had a passion and aptitude beyond his years.

In 1851, at the age of eighteen, Cyril's own grandfather had emigrated to Australia from the Isle of Man off the west coast of England to escape famine and a grasping stepmother. He had taken the farm's only handcart and, with his sea chest strapped on tight, made his way to port, never to return. The only difficult decision for him had been the destination, whether America, where his brother was bound, or Australia, from where fantastic reports were emerging of torrents of gold flowing up out of the ground. Family folklore has it that William Sr intended to return home a few years later when the recession was over and his fortune had been made.

Ballarat had been as easy to find as any promised land. He hitched a ride and joined the throng heading to the new El Dorado. He threw his hat in with a syndicate with six other miners drunk on the prospect of riches – the reality, however, was harsh. The paucity of strikes sent them traipsing west to harvest wheat in Victoria's Wimmera district before returning to try their luck afresh at Fiery Creek near Beaufort.

Finally, at the end of nearly a decade of toil and his own tether, William Sr struck just enough gold to go into business. In 1863 he married Rose, the seventeen-year-old daughter of his mining partner, and deployed his limited wealth into purchasing timber to sell to other miners for shoring up their shafts. It was sufficient to secure survival but the couple's home remained a tent among thousands of others and a million flies on the mud and clay.

Within a year the tenacious Manxman had saved enough to build a two-room timber dwelling on the banks of the Trawalla Creek near Chute. A story passed down through the family claims that on a visit to Melbourne he bought a block of land in Collins Street for £5, though he never secured the title and was relieved of his luggage by an unscrupulous innkeeper.

Times remained hard, but William Sr persevered, supplementing his business with nightshifts underground for the Royal Saxon Gold-Mining Company of Ballarat to support a family that would eventually number ten.

Many years later, in 1904, Cyril's father moved his family to the little town of Yendon, closer to Ballarat. Before long, however, his wife Rose contracted typhoid and became gravely ill. The disease, once known as 'colonial fever', had persisted in cities, towns and on the goldfields for decades.

At its worst, in the late 1880s, the typhoid death rate in Victoria was more than double that of England. It was referred to as the 'annual scourge' and summer was the 'typhoid season'. Caused by the ingestion of faeces-contaminated water and food, particularly milk and meat, the epidemic had been ably assisted by rudimentary sewerage systems that could not keep up with population growth, and a fly population that was stratospheric. Victims were capable of infecting many others before being diagnosed. Only one in ten cases were fatal, which gave the family some hope, but Rose was in such a poor state that the doctors gave her no chance of recovery. When she succumbed a short time later, her elder sister Eadie came to help with the children and she never left. It was rumoured that Aunt Eadie would have liked to have married William but his enduring affection for his late wife precluded it.

By the age of thirteen, Cyril's academic excellence had become evident to all. He won one of only forty Victorian state scholarships and his father enrolled him at Ballarat's leading private school, Grenville College. With no publicly funded secondary schools in existence, the scholarship was Cyril's only avenue to further formal education. The co-educational college accommodated boarders but a schoolteacher's wages wouldn't stretch that far, so Cyril moved into a rented house with his Uncle Cecil and his brother Reg, who was now attending the School of Mines. The boys slept on the front verandah, which was so cold in winter that if they slept with mouths open, it would be hours after they woke before their teeth stopped aching.

Founded in 1855, Grenville College offered a surprisingly liberal curriculum – courses in classics and mathematics were enhanced by teachers passionately versed in the arts and the school was renowned for turning out students of rare talent. Its alumni included the writer Mary Gaunt, radical poet Bernard O'Dowd and the son of a leader of the Eureka rebellion, Arthur Lynch, who had fought on the wrong side in the Boer War, been tried for treason and eventually entered the House of Commons.

Another bright boy of humble background commenced his schooling at Grenville the year after Cyril and, like him, boarded with relatives in Ballarat. Robert Gordon Menzies – 'Dag' as he was known to his schoolmates – was talkative and rambunctious, a direct contrast to Cyril's quiet reserve. While Cyril studied hard and reaped the rewards, the tall lay preacher's son from Jeparit would later confess to a lack of application that saw him nearly fail the leaving certificate.

In his first year at College, at the age of fourteen, my grandfather passed five of the six subjects required for university entrance. Although science remained his primary interest, he excelled in other disciplines as well, and the following year won a prize from the Melbourne Shakespeare Society. He travelled to the city and was presented with the award at a ceremony held at the Austral Salon of Music, Literature and the Arts. Cyril passed his examinations with ease but failed by a fingernail to gain the scholarship he needed for admission to the University of Melbourne.

His determination to succeed resulted in a year spent at the Ballarat School of Mines before repeating the exams and winning a government exhibition and residential scholarship to Queen's College. The delay meant that he would enter university in 1910 at the same time as his sister Alice, who was studying humanities.

Cyril's talents were quickly recognised and he was soon taken under the wing of the faculty dean, David Orme Masson. 'Ormie', as the less reverent and more familiar knew him, was a man of vast ability and confidence who inspired the adulation of his students. He took Cyril on as a research assistant and the student thrived conducting experiments under the professor's tutelage. It didn't matter if it was work on the composition of nitroglycerin or critical solution temperatures, Cyril not only understood the processes but, as Ormie furiously scribbled equations across the blackboard, he rapidly began to understand the science.

Cyril and Alice graduated together in 1913, but Cyril stayed on to complete his honours examination the following March. Masson's investment in the aspiring young chemist was repaid with interest – first class honours and the Dixon final honours exhibition. With Ormie's encouragement Cyril spent the rest of the year with research work at the university.

Cyril's brother Reg had completed his studies at the School of Mines and taken up a position assaying for a company on the Kalgoorlie goldfields in Western Australia. But by the time he arrived, the desert sands were no longer willingly giving up their riches and he was forced to find work as a labourer. Some time later he left for west Africa and took up work in a huge gold mine on the Gold Coast, where colonialists had been plundering the earth's reserves for centuries.

When the Archduke Franz Ferdinand was assassinated in June 1914, Reg was working deep underground. The Royal Prince of Hungary had actually visited Australia in the year of Cyril's birth, and Melbourne's *Argus* newspaper carried a report of him touring a meat preserving plant. Now, some twenty years later, his murder by Serbian radicals in Sarajevo was the catalyst for a series of events that would plunge the world into a war of unprecedented scale. It was weeks before Reg received word and made arrangements to return home.

As the conflict in Europe escalated, Britain called for sacrifice from every quarter of her Empire. The declaration of war on Germany from Westminster on 4 August 1914 had come in the midst of a hard fought Australian election campaign. There was bipartisan commitment to the defence of the realm; anything else would have been political suicide. As public nationalism surged, Prime Minister Joseph Cook and his Labor rival Andrew Fisher swore ever more patriotic vows of support.

'Our duty is quite clear,' Cook declared, 'to gird up our loins and remember we are Britons.'

Not to be outdone, his opponent swore to defend Britain 'to our last man and our last shilling'.

Within three months more than 20,000 Australian men

had volunteered. It seems the rush to defend the realm was as fevered as the one to dig for gold. Few had much idea of what they were signing up for but most were fearful of missing out on the chance to be part of a stoush that some predicted would be over by Christmas.

Cyril had completed his research work and had taken a position with a company in Fitzroy producing a hotchpotch of household goods and industrial products. His duties at Lewis & Whitty were disagreeable and mundane, often involving standing over various reeking vats bubbling with shoe polish, starch, soap or sheep dip. Each week the company's workforce diminished as men gladly traded the drear of factory life for an overseas adventure. My grandfather was keen to join them. He had hoped that his education might qualify him for officer's school but in early 1915, to his disappointment, word came that he had been refused on grounds of age. He enlisted a few weeks later.

It was rare that all the children could be found in the one place together, but in January 1915 they gathered at Shepparton in north-eastern Victoria. Their father had accepted a post as headmaster of the local high school. When they were all finally seated at the dinner table, William called for quiet. 'May the Lord watch over our boys and keep them safe …'

When he finished the silence hung in the air.

Reg had completed his basic training at the hastily constructed new camp just outside Melbourne at Broadmeadows and Cyril was to travel to Seymour, eighty kilometres further north, to undertake his own.

The following morning once everyone was dressed and prepared, the family set off as one for town. It was a surreal scene that was repeated across the country as men, many just boys, gathered to be farewelled by crowds that seemed to have materialised out of nowhere. Mayors recited speeches ringing with pride, duty and honour, while fathers' feet shuffled and mothers, unable to keep their falsely sworn promises, simply wept.

Cyril and Reg took with them mementos of family – childhood photographs tucked in their tunic pockets. They were resilient country boys, sons and grandsons of pioneers, born into hardship and raised on scarcity. Walking fifteen kilometres to barracks on arrival or, for that matter, going without food afterwards was not an ordeal. They knew little of what lay ahead, but everyone else knew that whatever was required of them would be met by their own hand.

The Devil's Porridge

At Seymour, just over a hundred kilometres north of Melbourne, Cyril enjoyed the company of the other recruits, but he soon began to tire of the endless succession of parades, bayonet practice, boot cleaning and drills. For him the biggest challenge of war to date was boredom. He was relieved then to be transferred to Broadmeadows, on the outskirts of the city, if only for the change of scenery.

The flat windswept plain was dotted with hundreds of tents and the odd prefabricated building. The heatwaves and dust storms of January were supplanted by a miserably wet early autumn. It was cold and the reclaimed paddocks were poorly drained. Lack of proper facilities at the makeshift camp resulted in an outbreak of influenza among the young troops.

The *Argus* newspaper reported that the field hospitals were inadequately prepared, theft was rife and that there were complaints about the quality of the food. The travelling kitchens, supplied at great expense to sustain the Light Horse Brigade, were declared useless on arrival by the quartermaster-general. After several months, public criticism became so great the Minister for Defence set up a Departmental Committee to investigate the claims.

When he wasn't marching or stabbing bags of straw in the rain, Cyril sought cover under one of the camp's big canvas marquees to read and write.

Before long, his brother Reg was gone, shipped out from Port Melbourne in May 1915 with an infantry battalion that had been formed only a month earlier. The week prior to departure had seen a frenzy of activity as officers gathered equipment and weeded out those men deemed sick or unfit. The underprepared force continued training on board as their troopship HMAT *Barambah* steamed beyond the equator towards the Suez Canal. The men slept on deck in hammocks slung from every available hitching point and spent their few leisure hours between parading and musketry complaining about the food and writing letters home. When the ship finally entered the Suez they saw their first active troops. Encampments of British and Indian forces were arrayed along the banks of the narrow man-made waterway. Two months earlier over two thousand Turkish soldiers had lost their lives in a failed attempt to seize control of the shipping lanes.

Reg and his company disembarked at the Egyptian port of Alexandria on the Mediterranean, journeyed by train and foot to camp and spent two months engaged in desert training exercises some twenty minutes outside the sprawling capital of Cairo. They returned to Alexandria at the end of August, as ready as they ever would be to cross the Aegean Sea and take on the might of the Ottoman Empire at Gallipoli.

When I was a child, I was told that my grandfather was scheduled to board a train from Broadmeadows with his brother Reg and ship out from Station Pier. The truth is, though, that at some point he was summoned by a senior officer who handed him his enlistment application.

Slashed across it in red pen was the word CANCELLED.

Cyril tried to argue his case with the authorities, without success. Soon, however, his old mentor Ormie Masson would come back into Cyril's life.

Masson was becoming very involved in the business of war and shared his clear-eyed vision with a Melbourne audience:

> Since the Great War began, two statements have been made, and so frequently repeated that today they are commonplace. The first is that the result … depends on … men and more men, munitions and yet more munitions. The second is that this is a war of chemists and engineers – a war of applied science.

Masson and his brilliant University of Melbourne colleague Professor William Osborne had already begun to prepare a list of those who would join their mission. Somewhere near the top was my reluctant grandfather. Cyril would not serve as a soldier but as a scientist.

The dangers of war were now becoming apparent. Already one schoolmate was dead. George Merz, the 1908 dux of

Grenville College, had completed his degree in medicine before enlisting and graduating top of his pilot's course. He was dispatched to Mesopotamia to fly reconnaissance missions for the British but soon found his medical skills were in greater demand. Apparently the dawn disappearance of his plane over Basra near Kuwait had followed a near sleepless night assisting overstretched hospital staff to tend the wounded. Merz was the first Australian aviator killed in war.

The munitions research plant to which Cyril was posted was hidden on a gentle curve of the Maribyrnong River, west of Melbourne. It resembled an island but for a ribbon of land connecting it to the bank.

The choice of the isolated location was no accident. Here would begin a secret war, as the scientific intellect of the Imperial forces attempted to rein in Germany's superiority in weapons manufacture. The first man to take up his station had a history in explosives. The next was Cyril, Ormie's man, and he was earmarked for training in the manufacture of cordite. The smokeless explosive was a gunpowder substitute, vital in propelling shells and cartridges.

Within a year my grandfather was transferred to England, where munitions production was in full swing. He was deployed as a chemist at an installation in northern Wales working twelve-hour shifts, seven days a week. It didn't trouble Cyril and his colleagues, whose appetite for work surprised their British counterparts, though they dubbed them 'those heathen Australians'. Once Cyril and his collegues had the Welsh plant running smoothly, it was handed over to British chemists. He was then informed that his talents were required elsewhere.

There had been strict secrecy surrounding the work in Wales, but now a new document was thrust in front of him that reflected the graver import of this new role. The place he was being sent was so crucial to the war effort that any disclosure would be viewed as an act of treason, punishable by death.

Reg couldn't feel his legs. He had gone from freezing to numb as he clung to a lifebuoy thrown from the troopship HMT *Southland*. Other survivors clung onto whatever floated the best. A few of the injured and lucky had scrambled into a handful of collapsible lifeboats. They had been in the water for over three hours. Before his unscheduled disembarkation, Reg remembered passing the isle of Rhodes as they steamed across the Aegean towards the Turkish Peninsula.

The troops of the 21st Battalion had been assembling on deck for ten o'clock parade on 2 September 1915 when several observed the German torpedo riffling the water's surface, racing towards the ship. It struck just forward of the bridge.

Reg was eventually plucked out of the water along with the other survivors and transferred to HMS *Transylvania*. The attack had taken forty of their number. The battalion's brigadier would later die from exposure suffered after his collapsible overturned.

For the living there was no time for recuperation. Two days later, in pitch-black darkness, the troops waded ashore at Anzac Cove. They were appalled at the tattered remnants of their compatriots. The following day they took up positions on the front line in rank muddy burrows they would call home for the next three and a half months. The trenches were two and a half feet wide by eight feet deep. There was no advance and no retreat. They suffered few casualties from enemy action but many fell sick through the constant work and scarce rations, reducing their fighting strength by a third. Men volunteered for the more dangerous beach fatigue party just to escape the hell of their holes in the ground. Conditions were deplorable but they knew, first-hand, that it was no better for the Turks. One October morning the constant howl of fire was briefly silenced while men from both sides came together to fraternise and exchange bully beef for Turkish tobacco and trifles.

As winter fell they dug in ever deeper, excavating a system of tunnels that would form their quarters. Their residence underground would be mercifully short. The bombardment of Lone Pine inflicted heavy casualties and finally, by mid-December 1915, the order was given and evacuation was underway. Only the most critically injured, however, would be returning home. Gallipoli had been the final chapter for so many unfortunate souls, but for Reg Callister and his brothers-in-arms this was merely the prologue. After a brief respite for Christmas on the Greek isle of Lemnos, they would set sail for the already bloodied battlegrounds of France.

My grandfather took a train from London's Euston Station and travelled north to the Scottish border. For hundreds of years the town of Gretna Green had also been the destination for young runaway English romantics escaping strict marriage laws. Blacksmiths' shops at the town's entrance had become the backdrop for hastily conducted nuptials, though no such romance greeted Cyril's arrival. Over the past year the once sleepy village had borne an incredible transformation as ten thousand labourers created a massive munitions installation that spread over thousands of acres.

In 1915, as British troops fell in France, the Minister for Defence, Lloyd George, sparked public outcry with his alarming report to the House of Commons on the munitions crisis. Germany's output of 250,000 high explosive shells per day was outstripping Britain's by a hundred to one. More disturbing facts emerged regarding the Empire's lack of battle capacity. No longer could Britain rely on superior strategy to outwit and outlast the enemy. It was said that at Waterloo it took one man's weight in lead to kill him. Now it was taking one hundred times that in projectiles. Munitions were the top priority and an escalation in production was essential.

Hiding a military installation of this scale from the enemy required a covert location and Gretna Green was identified as the ideal green field site. Enclosed by mountains and more often than not shrouded in rolling Scottish mist, it provided natural protection from attack. It was also serviced by the main Glasgow-to-London railway line.

The facility sprawled from the River Esk in the east to Dornock in the west. It branched out in all directions and from end to end spanned a distance of some sixteen kilometres. Other civil projects past and present paled into insignificance. It was an operation without precedent, a social experiment never previously conceived. Construction proceeded at a furious pace, much of it undertaken by Irish navvies lured by the prospect of higher than average wages. They were enthusiastic drinkers and pugilists and it was reported that their behaviour disturbed some of the more genteel locals. When their work was done, when the new schools, hospitals and housing had been erected, a labour force of thirty thousand descended on the Solway Firth, arriving almost as fast as her swift flowing tide. According to one observer the city became a virtual Babylon, home to people from all ends of the earth.

My grandfather stepped from the train and was swept down the Gretna Green platform with a large group of girls from the industrial town of Newcastle. Boisterous, amorous and as tough as the ashen factory-lined streets of their home, they would form an integral part of the new workforce. Cyril was not impressed, writing to his father that 'if Newcastle is to be judged by its women it must be a pretty poor shop'.

As the throng from the station fanned out, Cyril sought directions and made his way into the streets of the newly inflated town. Vast factory buildings surrounded by towering mounds of earth eventually gave way to the commercial buildings that would serve the new residents. Then more sprawling factories, their chimneys spewing smoke. Red skull and crossbone insignia marked the acid storage points, but the caustic odours alerted Cyril to their presence well before he saw the signs. The ubiquitous presence of fire hoses, water sources and brightly-coloured fire buckets clearly advertised the resident dangers. A constant stream of lorries and carts hauled cargoes of empty shell casings, soon to be filled. The bales of cotton piled up on one passing vehicle made my grandfather instantly homesick. Stencilled on their sides were the letters QLD AUS.

Cyril stopped to ask a farrier for directions and was pointed towards a factory and a flight of stairs. There he met with his English boss, Ferguson, who was straight to the point. Cyril was to be in charge of the gun-cotton section of His Majesty's Munitions Factory. No excuses were made for the risks, conditions or the accommodation, which Cyril soon discovered was spartan. The only defence against the freezing Scottish winter was a wood heater in the common area that provided plenty of smoke but very little heat.

The following morning Cyril went to work in an office-cum-laboratory raised up on a mezzanine to provide a clear view of the factory floor below. The lab was a basic affair with a porcelain sink, a bench, an empty bookshelf and a couple of stools. After a brief inspection he went down below and introduced himself to the workers. The heavy protective clothing and headgear they had been issued concealed any clue to their shape or gender.

Cyril began with an explanation of the composition and role of cordite. It was, he told his disguised audience, a simple combination of two highly explosive compounds, nitrocellulose and nitroglycerin. He then sought to assuage the anxiety he imagined on their faces by telling them that cordite was designed to burn rather than explode. Once the chemicals were mixed, the dry paste would be added to vats of surgically sterile batches of cotton. The resulting cordite would be spun into rods of varying thickness, the more rapidly burning narrow rods for use in small arms and the larger variety for artillery rounds.

The supply of clean, good quality cotton was essential. The slightest contamination, the smallest speck of dirt, could prove catastrophic when the benign fibre was soaked in the unstable, toxic brew.

Cyril tried his best not to overstate the dangers and frighten his new employees into flight, but the truth was the whole process required scrupulous care and a strong stomach. Danger at Gretna was as ever present as that on the front lines of war, and until the fighting stopped HMF Gretna Green would operate twenty-four hours a day, seven days a week. Indeed, as hostilities intensified, shell production rose to a staggering eight hundred tons per week. (At Maribyrnong, the target had been fifteen tons per year.) Arthur Conan Doyle, the inventor of Sherlock Holmes, visited Gretna Green in 1916 and was astounded:

> It is one of the wonder spots on earth … There the nitro-glycerin on the one side and the gun-cotton on the other are kneaded into a sort of devil's porridge … this by the way is where the danger comes in … and the girls will still smile and stir their devil's porridge but it is a narrow margin between life and death.

In his correspondence, like everyone else, Doyle referred to the factory by its codename 'Moorside'. To do otherwise would have been to invoke the potentially fatal penalties inscribed on Cyril's red form.

Across the Channel, a huge explosion followed by an artillery barrage signalled the commencement of the Somme offensive. Word sped to Gretna Green and first reports were not good. The Empire's troops were facing slaughter. Cyril had one thought and that was for his older brother.

As it transpired, it was not long before they were reunited, brought together by a rare and happily coincidental chance to take a short leave break in London. The brothers met in central London and, as was the fashion of the day, queued for well over an hour in a Regent Street photographer's to have their portrait taken. When it was their turn they were pushed and prodded into the appropriate pose. Cyril enclosed the photograph in an envelope and sent it home with a note saying that he liked 'the sitting one best'. But the respite was short-lived – Reg soon returned to battle and Cyril to his factory.

In the northern summer of 1916, Australia's troops received their baptism of fire on the Somme. In six weeks' fighting more would be killed than in the entire Gallipoli campaign. Reg and the 6th Machine Gun Company took up their position in the line behind the French town of Pozières. Australia's war historian Charles Bean would later write that it was 'a site more densely sown with Australian sacrifice than any place on earth'.

William received news of his son's wounding and immediately wrote for further information. But before he had received any response from the authorities, a letter arrived from Cyril, informing him that Reg had been awarded the Military Cross:

> For conspicuous good service since arrival in France. Under fire shows exceptional coolness and has set a very fine example to his men. Also for gallant and valuable work during period 26th to 28th at Pozières where he occupied a very exposed machine gun position which was continuously and heavily shelled. On the 28th of July, when his other section leader was badly hit Lieutenant Callister although himself wounded in the back remained at his post and carried on.

Reg's wounds were not severe and his time out of action brief. His exposure to the horrors of war motivated Cyril to work even harder, supervising activity on the factory floor beyond his shifts. Even the laziest of his team exerted themselves and the most diligent pushed beyond exhaustion.

Feminist and journalist Rebecca West also visited Gretna Green and observed that for many of the girls from impoverished backgrounds, the motivation of earning money was enough to keep them going.

> Every morning at six ... 250 of these girls are fetched by a light railway from their barracks on a hill two miles [three kilometres] away. When I visited ... they had already been at work for nine hours, and would work for three more. This twelve-hour shift is longer than one would wish, but it is not possible to introduce three shifts, since the girls would find an eight-hour day too light and would complain of being debarred from the opportunity of making more money ... The girls who take up this work sacrifice almost as much as men who enlist; for although they make on average 30s a week they are working much harder than most of them, particularly the large number who were formerly domestic servants, would ever have dreamed of earning in peacetime.

In the article West wrote for the *Daily Chronicle*, she reported something 'distinctly domestic' in the girls' daily routine.

> When one is made to put on rubber over-shoes before entering a hut it might be the precaution of a pernickety housewife concerned about her floors, although actually it is to prevent the grit on one's outdoor shoes igniting a stray scrap of cordite and sending oneself and the hut up to the skies in a column of flame. The girls who stand round the great drums in the hut with walls and floor awash look like millers in their caps and dresses of white waterproof, and the bags containing a white substance

that lie in the dry ante-room might be sacks of flour. But, in fact, they are filling the drum with gun-cotton to be dried by hot air. And in the next hut, where girls stand round great vats in which steel hands mix the gun-cotton with mineral jelly, might be part of a steam-bakery. The brown cordite paste itself looks as if it might turn into very pleasant honey-cakes; an inviting appearance that has brought gastritis to more than one unwise worker.

But how deceptive this semblance of normal life is; what extraordinary work this is for women and how extraordinarily they are doing it, is made manifest in a certain row of huts where the cordite is pressed through wire mesh. This, in all the world, must be the place where war and grace are closest linked. Without, a strip of garden runs beside the huts, gay with shrubs and formal with a sundial ... One girl stands high on a platform against the wall, filling the cordite paste into one of the two great iron presses, and when she has finished with that she swings round the other one on a swivel with a fine, free gesture. The other girls stand round the table laying out the golden cords in graduated sizes from the thickness of rope to the thinness of macaroni, the clear khaki and scarlet of their dresses shining back from the wet floor in a perpetually changing pattern as they move quickly about their work.

The living conditions for the girls was as basic as the work was brutal. One of the cordite workers reported that:

We lived in hostels, just wooden huts with long dormitories and a large living room ... (no comforts). Each girl had a small bedroom … it was very cold. We worked in three shifts and we went to work in trains. We changed into overalls and hats to cover all our hair and shoes that must not touch the ground outside where we worked. It was an awful job if on night shift – cold rain, dark and lonely, pushing the heavy trucks, and rats running around your feet. Sometimes the girls were drunk with fumes from the cordite and had to be taken to the sick bay to sleep it off.

In the few hours between sleep and work, those with any remaining strength took up the various opportunities Gretna furnished for recreation. The Ministry of Defence had provided numerous clubs and pubs for the purpose and other nearby towns where employees were lodged adjusted their businesses accordingly. It was rumoured that when five thousand workers arrived by train one night at an inn in Carlisle the publican had a thousand whiskies lined up ready on the bar.

From a letter to his father it seems Cyril was a reluctant participant in such frivolities.

> I was beguiled into attending another festivity in a girls' hostel on Thursday night, the mistletoe season is closed but its assistance doesn't appear necessary.

As it was, my grandfather met my soon-to-be grandmother not under the mistletoe but at work. Katherine Mundell was known to all as Kit and lived with her mother and sisters in a two-storey brick house in the centre of the Scottish town of Annan, about eight kilometres from the munitions factory.

Kit was thin with brown eyes and her dark hair fell straight to rest on her shoulders. Her father had been the local tailor, dying shortly before the war, and one of her brothers, George, took over the shop before leaving for France. Her eldest brother Percy travelled to the Far East, wrote a few letters home and was never heard from again. In October 1915 George went 'over the top' in the Battle of Loos and was one of the first to reach the German trenches before being killed. It was revealed later that his unit hadn't possessed enough artillery rounds.

As well as two brothers Kit had three sisters and it was with one of them, Hope, that she made her way to the Dornock end of the munitions factory once it was completed. She was given a job as secretary to an Australian chemist called Smith, who worked up at Acid Point, the place where the most toxic chemicals were made and stored. Kit's friend Agnes was later assistant to my grandfather and soon they were all acquainted. It wasn't long before Cyril began calling on Kit at home – even for the painstaking chemist, war served as a constant reminder not to waste time.

In his letters home, Cyril divulged little information about their courtship, no doubt a matter that he thought would be considered frivolous in the face of his brother's travails in France:

> Things are not progressing satisfactorily … The weather in Flanders for the last offensive has simply been vile and quite apart from the additional strain on the men, it plays 'Old Harry' with the transport and aerial work. Of course it worries Fritz too but he's got solid ground and years of organization behind him, and our people have nothing but miles of quagmire and devastation. Not withstanding, Fritz continues to get it well and truly in the neck. And

it can't encourage him a horrible lot …The Yanks really mean business and there are a large number of their raw, untrained but very cocky troops on the Salisbury Plain at present. There are also some in France and one of the A.I.F recently told me that a party of Yanks had encountered some of our troops in Boulogne. Each crowd was rather curious to see the other and the Australian spokesman enquired of the Yanks their reason for troubling themselves in coming to France.

"'Wal", we have come along here to do what you chaps can't' was the reason given. Then there was a brief civil war in the allied army resulting in a number of the Yanks being severely handled. They keep the Yanks away from us in France now, said my informant. I don't know why. I don't know why I should endeavour to write like a military expert, it is very difficult to get reliable information. This I do know, that the war is going on until the Germans are hammered out as flat as a sardine tin and that we are going to do it. Industrially if we only use a little common sense after the war they are ruined …

Cyril was at pains to play down the dangers of his own position:

With regard to blowing up factories Krupps is completely overshadowed by munitions works plastered all over the country. And they take a lot of stopping. Explosives factories are always built with a view to possible accidents, and it is only rare as at Silvertown that a single explosion can wreck a whole factory.

At the Silvertown munitions factory in Essex in early 1917 the explosion of fifty tons of TNT had killed seventy-three and injured four hundred. Other major explosions had occurred in Faversham and Chilwell but no official acknowledgement of the fatal disasters had been made.

> My job is regarded in explosive circles as absolutely safe. The one I was on up to last Christmas was not. So you need not have any worry on that score. That's rather a confession to make when all one's pals and eligible relatives are fighting, but it's true never the less. If an explosion occurred on our joint, I guess yours truly would be looking for a new job about the next day or two.

Cyril then turned to news of home, where railway workers were on strike and the Roman Catholic Archbishop Mannix was stirring the pot against conscription. When it was claimed that Catholics were not doing their share, the Irishman retorted that 'apparently not enough nuns are joining up'. Hardened by his proximity to danger, my grandfather suggested some effective, if unconventional, means of solving the issues:

> There appears to be another bad strike on in Australia, railways this time. The best means of curing them would be to return one of the Australian divisions to deal with them. Also can't somebody shoot Mannix. If he is so anxious to be a martyr, I've no doubt Melbourne could stand him a nice funeral. The RC's are making a lot of trouble in Canada over the conscription question. Mainly the French Canadians according to report. The Roman

element isn't much use to the empire. The pope seems to have got his fingers burnt over his latest peace muddle. There's one thing about that crowd, they always make beaucoup trouble for themselves when it isn't necessary. This is not a political discourse, so I will close.

As a postscript, Cyril chivvied his father for some or other self-effacing remark:

I don't like the poor old country schoolmaster touch I guess you have turned out a lot of good Australians in the last 30 yrs and that's something to have lived for. If I can show as good a record when I'm your age I'll be satisfied.

Love and War

At the entrance to the munitions factory in the south London district of Woolwich, a guard checked over Cyril's papers and instructed him to stay put until his escort arrived. Beyond a high brick wall a persistent growl of machinery was punctuated by the thunder of heavy weaponry. After a brief wait, a tall fellow with a black stub of moustache – a reverse-engineered replica of his father – appeared at the gate. His handshake relayed a compatriot's warmth.

As they walked, David Ormie Masson's son, Irvine Masson, congratulated Cyril on his appointment as official representative of the Chemical Institute of Australia.

Like Gretna Green, the Royal Arsenal was a vast munitions development and testing facility that ranged over some thirteen hundred acres. Situated on the southern bank of the River Thames and originally known as the Woolwich Warren, it had grown and shrunk and grown again since the late seventeenth century, mirroring the nation's fortunes at war. It had also once been the location of the great wooden prison hulks that housed convicts in chains prior to their transportation to Australia. Now it was a labyrinth of low-rise buildings and reclaimed swamplands, teeming with military activity.

Irvine asked Cyril if he had ever seen any of his ordnance in action. He hadn't.

'You've come on the right day.'

He handed Cyril a pair of earplugs. They stood with other observers near the gunnery sergeant, who immediately issued commands to his crew. A six-inch shell was rammed into the Howitzer and the firing plate slammed shut.

The order to fire was given and a shock wave hit Cyril's chest. Even with the earplugs jammed in tight, the noise was incredible. He noticed that one of Irvine's colleagues clicked his stopwatch, timing the shell's flight to impact. Soon after there was a puff of white smoke and the tell-tale upsurge of dirt.

Irvine tapped Cyril on the shoulder and gestured for him to remove his earplugs. 'We've got to test a few rounds from the Holton Heath Naval Cordite Factory. Then it's your turn.'

Cyril flinched. The last thing he wanted to see was a dud produced from his own factory.

As they watched the gun crew preparing the next round of charges, Irvine described life at the Royal Arsenal. More than eighty thousand people were stationed there and a housing estate had been constructed at nearby Eltham to accommodate the growing army of workers. Irvine found it challenging and exciting, a welcome change from University College in London. He asked after Cyril's cousin Colin whom Cyril had visited in hospital en route to Woolwich. The man had been hit running into his own brigade's barrage during the confusion and uproar of an attack, something he had told Cyril was very difficult to avoid. Afterwards he had lain in the rain for three days before being picked up by the stretcher-bearers. A fragment of shell had pierced his skull and the doctor told Cyril that Colin was lucky to have survived.

They waited for the next blast, now more than ever aware of the damage the munitions they developed were causing other men, even their own. Yet Cyril the scientist just hoped the charges he had developed at Gretna Green, fuelled by the temperamental gun-cotton, would pass testing. Remarkably, that afternoon at Woolwich was the first time he had seen any artillery fired. It was not for him to pass judgment on their final deployment and he rarely allowed himself the indulgence of pondering the results of his work.

To his relief there were no duds. A number of the other rounds failed, but he knew it was more luck than anything else. Sometimes up to thirty per cent of all ordnance refused to detonate.

Cyril departed the Woolwich Warren without enthusiasm. His munitions might have met the mark, but after two and a half years of war there was no end in sight and the work with cordite would continue for who knew how long. The only thing that cheered his spirits was a reunion with his Scottish sweetheart.

On his return to Gretna Green, Cyril made his way up the staircase to his office, where Kit's friend Agnes enquired about

Modest beginnings. *From left*: Cyril's grandfather William Sr, grandmother Jessie, aunt Emily, father William and, standing, sister Florrie, on the verandah at Chute in 1915. *Below*: The house in the mid-1980s.

William Callister, Cyril's father, in 1911. This picture may have been taken at the Ballarat School of Mines laboratory.

Cyril's mother, Rosetta, known to all as Rose.

Some of the Callister children *(left to right)*: Reg, Alice, Cyril,
Ruby and Minnie in front, around the turn of the century.
Allan, Florrie, Edie and Ralph missed out on this occasion.

A very proud Alice and Cyril on their graduation from
the University of Melbourne, 1914.

Reg and Cyril had their portrait taken during a brief
furlough in London, 1916.

Senior executive staff of the Kraft Walker Cheese Company, c. 1926.
Theo Easton stands top left, then A. R. Caughey (marketing) and C. H. Mason,
who would later become md. Cyril is seated next to a resplendent Fred Walker
in dazzling white. Frederick Sheppherd sits on Fred's left, and became
company secretary in 1930.

Courtesy of Kraft Foods Australia

his trip. The three older lab technicians acknowledged their boss's return with relief and trepidation. Thick glass bottles of acid, ether and other volatile substances crowded the laboratory benches. They were accompanied by cotton samples and the shelves above were piled with rows of bound files. Cambridge mathematics whizzes had been recruited to track, measure and account for everything related to the enterprise of war. Nothing was left to chance. Successes were meticulously documented, failures even more so. New processes were constantly being developed to attempt to meet the demands of the military machine. The pace was fast and methodical. When shortcuts were made, the consequences were dire.

On occasion, when the tall factory doors had to be suddenly swung open to cool a dangerously overheated brew, Cyril would gather his team together to deliver a speech light on words but bright with anger. His workers looked at their boots as he spoke. My grandfather was demanding and unrelenting and he expected a lot more than some were able to give. Even so, he also championed their cause. Gretna Green was the only munitions plant at the time that was still enforcing twelve-hour shifts. While some workers were desperate for money and reluctant to relinquish any extra hours, others were becoming rundown and sick. Cyril took the issue to his superiors and argued for his workers but he met with little success.

Over in Europe, Captain Reg Callister had spent the summer and autumn of 1917 moving north from the Somme in France to Flanders and then to Ypres in Belgium. As winter fell he returned to the Somme. It was a ceaseless procession by foot from one hell to another and back again and was taking such a toll, Reg reported that even 'staunch men had to be urged to leave the dug-outs'. Even where the guns were silent, the relentless grind of war bore down.

For Cyril, the winter of 1917–18 brought freezing temperatures. New hazards arose in the factory. The floor that was almost always wet with water was transformed into an ice rink. Some of the girls fell heavily, breaking bones and suffering concussion.

Cyril tried in vain to gain pay increases for his scientific colleagues, whose work he believed wasn't receiving the respect or reward it deserved. A letter was eventually tabled in the British Parliament but the fact remained that a considerable percentage of the tradesmen employed at Gretna Green were paid more than the chemists. Even so, Cyril wrote to his father that not all of his colleagues had earned the respect they believed they were owed:

> We have an insect from Nottingham named Williams. He who has been an infant prodigy, I think, is unlikely to recover from the excessive swell of the head in consequence. He has the nerve to have his letters addressed Mr Gill Williams B Sc 1st Class Honours London. We are thinking of buying some insectibane for it.

Other workers struggled to meet Cyril's strict requirements. His challenge was to recruit a skilled labour force drawn from a pool of some of the poorest and most under-educated regions of Britain. The first batch of girls he had trained he described as having only 'a rudimentary intelligence' for the job, relying heavily on Matron to groom them. She quietly moved aside girls who couldn't cope. But then, to Cyril's anger, Matron herself was moved on, taking some of the girls with her.

On one occasion while walking home from work Cyril was buttonholed by a stranger.

''Ere you,' the man said. 'What's with the missus losing her job? You've no right.'

A young woman stood nervously in the shadows. Cyril recognised her at a glance and composed himself. 'The contraband checks are done for good reason. After repeated breaches your wife continued to disregard the warnings. Matches, buttons, then something else the next week. She was reprimanded, warned and then I was left with no choice.'

'But you've no right,' countered the woman's husband.

'She doesn't have the attitude for the job.'

He later wrote to his father that such explanations 'did not appear to meet with much favour'.

Kit was Cyril's one salvation from the stresses of factory life. Her cheerful spirits and sing-song Scots accent captivated him and, amid the turmoil and tedium, she provided colour and light.

Matron was moved to Acid Point, where Kit worked and sulphuric acid was produced and stored. There the odour leached into air and hair and was impossible to get used to.

Cyril was at his desk when the explosion occurred. Windows shook with its violence and girls screamed. The faces of his colleagues distorted in silent fear. Someone below yelled for calm but the workers rushed to escape. Others moved quickly to their safety positions. Cyril checked on the factory floor before following. As they waited for the danger of secondary blasts to pass it became clear that the direction in which the explosion happened was up near Acid Point. Cyril's fears redoubled.

Even in winter, the heat from the blast site was so extreme that it was two days before anyone could get close. Earth bunkers surrounding the warehouse had contained most of the smouldering debris, preventing a massive inferno that might have incinerated all of Gretna Green. Reports were heavily censored because of security risks but according to one worker:

> When the girl was killed I was on the day shift and I was in bed at home. We heard the explosion all the way from there ... we went outside the door and could see the flames rising all the way from Annan.

An investigation revealed that a young girl late for her shift had run past a rubber bag on the ground and unknowingly flicked dirt onto the gun-cotton, which was soon after added to a nearby vat. The hot batch was detected too late.

Somehow Matron managed to get her girls out but was herself caught in the subsequent explosion. It wasn't clear if she was still looking for one of the workers. No one would ever know. Cyril's superiors were satisfied that their safety measures had prevented a catastrophe but he didn't share their joy.

On a June afternoon Reg Callister marched into the grounds of a small chateau west of Villers-Bretonneux in northern France. The river Somme lapped a corner of the chateau's wall where a large group of Australian soldiers, some still clad in field gear, swam and shouted. Others looked on, propped against stone warmed by late afternoon sun. The war that was going to be over by Christmas had now persisted for four years. Victory at Amiens and Villers-Bretonneux had provided a glimmer of light at the end of a long tunnel. To the north-east the Australian General John Monash was finalising elaborate plans for an attack on the town of Hamel.

A few days later Reg and his company were ordered back into the line, and as they came into position, overlooking Monument Wood, his company moved up beside the Zouaves. These were North African soldiers of the French army. One of Reg's mates wrote that the men were

> mostly friendly, offering us part of their rations. The Zouaves received a wine ration and the rate of exchange was one Australian clasp knife to one petrol tin of vin rouge. Until the clasp knives gave out.

Events on the Western Front were hastening towards an armistice but near Hamel the shelling was heavy.

Reg was proceeding to a gun position when he was hit.

> Captain Callister was … struck by a small fragment of a 4.2 shell which went through and out of the triceps of his left arm. The medical officer of the 23rd Battalion injected anti-tetanus serum and its effects were worse than those of the shell splinter. As on a previous occasion when wounded at Pozières, Captain Callister carried on and made little reference to his injury.

While on a cycling excursion near Gretna Green my grandfather told Kit that he was being transferred. Now as they waited at the station his sullen quiet prompted her to nervous chatter. She didn't cry until Cyril's carriage was out of sight.

At London's Euston Station, Cyril was bustled along by a herd of servicemen lugging kit and rifles out under the massive iron arch to the street. He bypassed the waiting cabs and joined the flow of pedestrians. It was slow going and his arms ached as he half-carried, half-dragged his chest. Finally, in Gower Street, he arrived at the gates of University College London.

Dr Harker's assistant greeted Cyril and, after brief small talk, moved to the job at hand – nitrogen fixation. Across the quadrangle stood a new building housing the Munitions Inventions Research laboratory where Cyril would work. His lodgings were a few kilometres away in St John's Wood. Despite Kit's absence, it felt exciting, a refreshing change from Gretna Green. He loved strolling the Bloomsbury district around the university and visiting Camden Lock on his day off.

The work was as hectic as anticipated and Dr Harker had gathered together a number of distinguished scientists. Some had military rank and were seconded from the army, but all had undertaken significant research in the fields of physics and chemistry. Despite their credentials, they were shadowing the advances made by the Germans. The chemist Fritz Haber had collaborated with industrialist Carl Bosch to pioneer a method of developing a synthetic fertiliser. This scientific breakthrough also had a more sinister application – the use of ammonium nitrate in munitions manufacture.

Cyril was astounded at the sophistication of the laboratory at his disposal, but the science of nitrogen fixation was relatively

simple – unlike the mechanics of the process, which were challenging and dangerous. A metal catalyst was added to nitrogen
and hydrogen at a temperature of 400 degrees centigrade to
make liquid ammonia. Depending upon which way you applied
the result, one of Cyril's colleagues noted, you could either have
lovely geraniums or a bloody big hole in the ground.

The scientists seconded from the army were intimately
acquainted with the progress in other laboratories across the
US, Europe and, in particular, Germany. In their company Cyril
became party to scientific developments of critical secrecy and
military importance.

In October 1918, Dr Harker entered the research laboratory
with the news that it was time for a change of scenery. A new
factory, a new job, more experience. It didn't matter that Kit
was coming down to London. Cyril managed to get a quick
message to her sister Leena:

> Have left London for the time being. Will contact with
> details love Cyril.

This was to be only the briefest of postings. Only a few
weeks later a vast throng surged into Trafalgar Square, to join
others who had gathered throughout the day. Most were deliri-
ous, some were dumbstruck. The war was over.

Reg and the other exhausted diggers had been pulled out
of the front lines before the armistice was announced. The
authorities thought that they had already done enough.

When Cyril met Kit at Euston Station, he told her that he
had been ordered to take charge of a new factory at Stratford.
It wouldn't happen now. He also told her that he wanted to go

home and that he wanted her to go with him.

They married in Annan in March 1919. Cyril's best man was Robert Summers, the scientist he had met four long war years earlier in Maribyrnong. Kit's sister Leena was bridesmaid. The couple departed England soon after the wedding, but their honeymoon was brief. The Australian Arsenal Branch had one last demand of him – a detour to America on a fact-finding mission. This meant that my grandfather was only able to bring his new wife home six months later.

Cyril and Fred

As the ship steamed through the grey murk of Melbourne's Port Phillip Bay, Station Pier grew from a distant thin line to a looming welcome to land. Except for one or two low buildings behind it, it was difficult to see any sign of a city through the drizzle. A harbour pilot had boarded the vessel outside the heads but passengers anxiously watched on as tugboats nudged it to rest alongside a wharf that was really too small for a modern steamship.

As the operation neared completion, the first of the celebratory streamers was cast from an upper deck but fell short and collapsed into the water. My grandfather's fared better, gently snaking its way down to the wharf's edge to land at the feet of a wildly waving family.

It wasn't his. After the rush of disembarkation, Cyril established that Kit's new in-laws were nowhere to be seen. Although Kit had frequently raised the topic of his family, she had prised little out of him. When, in a casual moment, she managed to dislodge a few small details, her new husband intimated that his father was somewhat strict and demanding. Reluctantly Cyril had shown Kit some photographs and, after learning of the loss of his mother, she felt she understood something of his reticence to reveal more. She knew that his family had little money. All else was left to piece together from conversations with Reg and his English fiancée May.

Kit finally met her in-laws after a long trip to Shepparton. She felt it a somewhat stiff affair and Cyril's father was still the local school principal there. Nevertheless, she immediately identified the greatest similarity between the two men – their intense spirit of enquiry.

Soon after their return to Melbourne and after settling in to comfortable bayside Brighton, the military called my grandfather in to begin the exhausting process of debriefing.

They commenced with the scouting work he had just undertaken in America. This was almost exclusively concerned with the treatment of timber for manufacturing aircraft, a somewhat obscure challenge for a chemist more familiar with food and munitions. His interrogators quizzed him for every detail: specific processes, stress levels, failure rates. The list was exhaustive but Cyril was equal to the task.

After a week or so they moved on to the gas. Cyril hated even talking about the use of gas as a weapon. In Germany, too, there had also been many who despised it. Clara Haber, whose husband Fritz was known as the father of chemical warfare, had taken her own life in protest only days after chlorine was first used on the western front. Cyril spoke about the impact of liquid bromide – the irksome but non-lethal tear gas – before detailing the deadly horrors of phosgene and mustard gas.

Trench warfare followed. Cyril told them what he'd learned from Reg and from interviews he had completed at the Department's request, which allowed him to paint a graphic picture. He was more engaged when talking about the science of nitrogen fixation, but still they moved him on. Finally, after weeks of inquisition and talk, they arrived at the subject of which my grandfather had the most intimate knowledge: the perils of cordite manufacture. He took them on a wide-ranging tour of Gretna Green. The munitions complex had cost over £9 million to build and, by the end of the war, £12 million to operate. Cyril was thorough, releasing an ocean of research, recommendations and opinions, sparing them nothing. By March 1920 though, he, and they, had had enough.

His war was finally over, but the city streets that had rejoiced at armistice were now robbed of joy by the presence of those same men in civilian clothes begging the price of a meal. The suffering of war had been quickly replaced by the Spanish flu pandemic, a disease that had originated in Kansas in America and was more correctly named pneumonic influenza. The highly contagious disease attacked healthy young adults and had seen Melbourne's Royal Exhibition Buildings – site of the first Federal Parliament in 1901 – turned into a makeshift hospital. By the time it had run its course, Spanish flu had killed over twenty million people worldwide – more than all of World War I. In Australia more than ten thousand people died of the illness within a twelve-month period. Between war and disease, there had been no rest from grief.

Fortunately my grandfather had a job to return to at Lewis & Whitty and a new life before him – even if its precise route was uncertain. Cyril had education and experience to draw on and a loving wife to support and care for.

Melbourne would soon begin its postwar boom and the modernisation of the heart of the city had already commenced, but the antiquated premises of Lewis & Whitty were in the grimy, unkempt backstreets of inner-city Fitzroy.

Cyril detected the soap fumes through the smog long before he reached his destination. He passed the huddled, dwarfish workers' dwellings, many of which shared a common wall with factories, workshops and warehouses. There was nothing modern here. The scene was Victorian in the mid-nineteenth century sense and Gretna Green seemed positively futuristic by comparison. He turned into Charles Street, walked a short distance and in through the familiar doors of the triple-storeyed manufactory.

He was delighted to find that he was warmly welcomed, but surprised to discover that, apart from the notable absence of a few former colleagues, the factory had scarcely changed. The only difference was that it was producing an even wider assortment of items. Lewis & Whitty's catalogue now included vanilla essence, boric acid and harvester oils. The laboratory he had proudly designed now seemed – by his own appraisal – pathetic. It was as though they had been waiting for him to bring it up to scratch again.

His first task was to equip the laboratory for the refinement of existing lines and the investigation of new ones. He began with the vanilla extract, designing equipment including an ingenious percolator to extract the essence from the beans more efficiently. After his experiences with cordite their aroma was a more than pleasant change.

It was not long before Cyril had also become re-acquainted with Ormie Masson. His mentor was delighted with the news that Cyril had managed to find himself a 'Scottish lass' and pleased to hear they were expecting a child. The professor had met his own wife in Scotland, where he had grown up and attended university in Edinburgh with luminaries such as Arthur Conan Doyle. Ormie told Cyril that his son Irvine, to his relief, had moved back to University College in London. He had never been comfortable with the dangers that the Woolwich Warren presented.

With a secure job and hopes for a future uninterrupted by war, my grandfather's children came in fast succession. Jean, a blue-eyed, dark-haired girl, was first. Two years later Ian arrived and finally, a year after that, my father. He was named William Hugh after his grandfather, but as he grew he simply became Bill.

During this period Kit's sister Hope also emigrated to Australia. Hope had spent the immediate postwar years working as a nursing aide with terminally ill children in London. Cyril had kept up correspondence with her and, it seems, encouraged her to move to Australia, but there was some mystery surrounding the circumstances. On the boat out, Hope had met an Australian military officer to whom she became engaged, but the wedding plans were broken off by the time she arrived in Melbourne. Instead she married another man, Jack Van Steveren, and the couple settled in his hometown of Shepparton.

In the same year that my father was born, his father Cyril was lured away to take up a position with an intriguing, charming and successful entrepreneur. It was the biggest risk of his life. At Gretna Green, daily surrounded by deadly compounds, he had never dared take risks. Besides doing his best to carry out his commission and preserve the safety of his workers there had been few real decisions that were his to make. The necessities of war had dictated his every step and all voluntary action, fear even, was suppressed in the cause of duty. Now, somewhat anxiously, he was about to embark on a journey entirely of his own choosing. If he failed, the failure would be his own, but as he stepped inside the foyer of the new factory in South Melbourne for his interview, the thought provided him with a measure of courage. After cooking up the devil's porridge, what could be left to fear?

The meticulously groomed man who appeared before him was physically impressive – tall with a high forehead and luxuriant eyebrows. Without yet saying a word he also seemed more engaging than any businessman Cyril had ever met. His manner exuded sincerity and resolve. Smiling, Fred Walker shook his new chemist's hand.

My grandfather liked him immediately.

Unlike Cyril, Walker had been born into comfort, though that was all soon to change. A brother died at birth before Fred started school and then, a few years later, his father was crushed to death by factory machinery in a terrible accident. Fred was sent to the local state school and, although bright enough to secure a scholarship to a private institution, prematurely traded his academic prospects for work to help support his family.

The company that hired him had already made a name for itself in the food industry and was thriving on export trade. As agents for a Queensland meat company, John Bartram & Sons sold canned and frozen meat, but their specialty was preserved dairy and pork products: cheese, bacon, hams and butter packed into cans fitted with key-opening lids. Like Henry Jones with his fruit preserving business in Hobart, John Bartram & Sons exploited every opportunity. Canning goods for export was a lucrative business and Bartram's markets stretched from the Orient to Africa.

Fred saw potential in the food trade. After only a few years at Bartram's he quit and shipped out to Hong Kong to set up his own company. There among the expatriate British, savvy Chinese and thousands of other fortune-hunters attracted by the heady mix of cheap labour, free trade and commercial possibility, Fred Walker set about making his mark. He stayed for five years, some more successful than others, but by the time he returned to Melbourne he knew more about the world than most commercial men in the city.

In 1910 he commenced trading among the merchants in Flinders Street, importing and exporting an eclectic, diverse range of products, including racehorses and jockey silks. But the real money-spinner remained dairy foods and the grail was a cheese that would travel without mouldering or taint.

After much experimentation and failure, Fred managed to produce a resilient potted cheese and christened it Red Feather. It was made by embalming cheddar with sodium sulphate, grinding it to a paste and packing it into vacuum-sealed cans. Although it was not the runaway success the entrepreneur had hoped for, it allowed him to continue to seek new opportunities.

In Fred Walker's world, it seemed happiness was always closely followed by tragedy. In 1913, the year of his marriage, his younger brother died from peritonitis. A few years later Fred's wife May gave birth to their only child, Sheila. She was to become his constant companion and a familiar face to his workers.

After war broke out, Fred joined the militia and achieved the rank of captain, and became aide to John Monash, a position once occupied by Fred's father-in-law. Monash would rise to the heights but, as the war escalated, Fred was denied active service due to his essential role in the food industry. It was a sign of his success, but Fred was bitterly disappointed.

Fred Walker's grandson told me an interesting story about his grandfather and Monash. It had entered Melbourne folk-lore and, like all things that pass through lips, there were many varied accounts.

Shortly before the war Fred took Monash to the Australian Club in William Street in the heart of Melbourne. It was similar to any gentlemen's establishment of the day, a place where privileged men could go in privacy to discuss business, politics or sport – or steal away to smoky corners to mock the indis-cretions, commercial and otherwise, of their fellow members. Social tolerance was a low priority in the members' code of conduct.

After a pleasant lunch, Monash and Walker walked up William Street and parted company. On returning to his office, Fred found a handwritten note on his desk: *Don't ever bring another Jew to this club again.*

And Fred never did ... he never returned.

The war years were challenging for Fred Walker and his fledgling company. Improvements in canning and refrigeration made the export of products possible to all corners of the globe. German U-boat fleets soon targeted merchant shipping, however, seeking to deny supplies of essential goods to their enemies' citizens. As a result, the supply of many products became unreliable and some were simply unobtainable. Imported items like tea, coffee, tobacco and chocolate were rationed. Long after conflict ceased the demand for many food products far exceeded supply.

The shortages were a source of continual frustration for the public but Fred spotted opportunities. The popular British product Bovril – the 'beef tea' which had famously sustained not only British troops but Ernest Shackleton's exploration party as they traversed the Antarctic ice – inspired him to investigate a replica meat extract that could be mixed up as a hot drink. By the end of the war Fred's factory began producing Bonox and it was soon moving off grocers' shelves in unanticipated quantities.

The key to Bonox's success was capitalising on the lack of available fresh meat to sustain a robust diet. Even for those lucky few fortunate enough to find or afford a cheap cut of beef or mutton, the absence of domestic refrigeration meant that it would likely spoil in no time at all. The brown liquid, on the other hand, was professed to have a host remarkable qualities beyond that of a mere meat substitute. It was nothing short of 'fluid life' that would 'fill your veins with rich red blood'.

Upon drinking the miraculous meat broth, it was purported that:

All lassitude disappears. Hope takes the place of hope-lessness. Courage the place of fear. You're seized with the will to do things.

Bonox also cured the mysterious 'brain fag'. What was more, Fred's newspaper ads proclaimed that Bonox was 'pre-digested', so your body didn't have to labour to obtain the nutrients it needed. The message might have been hard to stomach but the product was going down well. So nutritious was Bonox that it was sold from pharmacists.

The slogan 'Coffee, Tea or Bonox' was pitched to the public and soon caught on. Walker's cramped headquarters in the vaults below the new train viaduct in Flinders Street could not keep pace with demand. In 1918 a company store was opened in Pitt Street, Sydney, and in the following year branches sprang up in Adelaide and New Zealand. It was apparent that Fred Walker was a man whose veins ran red with the steely stuff only Bonox could instil.

In early 1920, Walker made a bold move to further expand operations, and new premises, the site of a former co-educa-tional college, were secured and refitted in South Melbourne. But no sooner was production underway than it became clear that Fred had spread his assets too thinly. The company was still trading in a baffling inventory of products that, alongside butter, cheese and dripping, included rabbit skins and paper, petrol, tyres and trucks.

Bonox may have seemed a miracle cure, but the turmoil of postwar economic readjustment now saw Fred Walker's export interests begin to fail. To make matters worse, a rogue employee manipulated Fred's profit share scheme and illegally stripped the company coffers of £4000. Due to difficulties with refrigeration, even the rabbit skin business went bad. Credit became increasingly difficult to secure and by early 1922 Fred had amassed a startling £80,000 of debt.

The entrepreneur was too proud to retreat but not too proud to seek assistance. He called upon the favour of his financially astute city brethren and, in the face of liquidation, persuaded the National Bank of Australasia to help him out. The bank insisted that he appoint a prominent accountant as chairman of the reformed company and its two largest creditors were granted directorships in return for forgiving payment of debts.

None of this, however, tempered Fred's commercial zeal. He began to investigate the possibility of mimicking another British success called Marmite, a salty paste born of spent brewer's yeast. It was popular, but became scarce in Australia during the war when it was rationed to troops as a preventative to beriberi and scurvy.

An attempt was made to fill the void by Carlton & United Breweries, who used their own waste product to create a product called Cubex. The name stood for 'Carlton United Brewing Extract' but, despite advertisements that claimed it was 'better than beef tea' and could cure skin ailments, the thick bitter liquid failed to excite consumers.

The agency to distribute Marmite in Australia was owned by Sanitarium Health Foods, a Seventh Day Adventist-operated vegetarian food company that had first been established in Sydney at the turn of the century. Sanitarium had won the rights to distribute Marmite against fierce competition from other Australian companies. Its primary use was not as a sandwich spread but as a substitute for meat extract in flavouring broths and stews.

The success of Bonox had convinced Fred of the customer's growing appetite for healthy – and long-lasting – foodstuffs. The war may have been over but malnutrition remained the root of a large number of diseases, including rickets and goitre, particularly among infants and children.

The challenge of perfecting methods of preserving food remained. Products that wouldn't rot, spoil or decay from the moment they were loaded onto trucks or put into the pantry had the potential to sell well. Domestic refrigerators had been produced and sold in America since 1918, but the kerosene-powered machines were astronomically expensive in Australia and used highly toxic chemicals as a refrigerant. A few imported demonstration models from companies such as Kelvinator had reached Australian shores, but for the most part the idea of keeping foodstuffs fresh in anything but an icebox remained a novelty. So new was the concept that a special glass-walled refrigerator was designed as the centrepiece of the Australian Pavilion at the 1924 British Empire Exhibition in London. In it were displayed carcasses of mutton and other perishable products, including specimens of Australian native flowers and fish frozen in blocks of clear ice. When Queen Mary stopped by the Pavilion on a surprise visit, she made flattering comment on the huge three-pound pears stored within.

Fred Walker was clever enough to realise that if he was to succeed in developing new foodstuffs and compete with the imports, he needed more than just a new factory. The most popular imported goods were protected by patent. Fred needed a chemist capable of unravelling the molecular mysteries of the base ingredients and transmuting them into palatable, preservable – and, most importantly – saleable products.

On that first meeting at the factory, Fred gave my grandfather a cursory rundown of the merits and weaknesses of Walker company products. Before long he arrived at the real object of his conversation. He looked Cyril in the eye and asked him what he knew of the properties of brewer's yeast.

As science went, the nutritional merit of yeast was a relatively new concept. The pioneering Frenchman Louis Pasteur had concluded in 1857 that yeast cells were a living organism. Cyril explained to Fred that an obscure Polish biochemist named Casimir Funk had made some newer advances in food science and in 1912 had coined the word 'vitamin'.

He also told Fred that scientists had been fiddling around with the spent product of brewing since the late 1680s with varying results. 'It's quite a process,' he added.

Later that day Cyril caught the tram back to his home in Brighton. Over the dinner table he quietly announced that he was now the new head chemist at Fred Walker & Company.

His daughter looked at him, eyes wide.

'Do they make chocolate?'

A disappointing 'no' was the reply.

His wife took up the chase.

'So how many other chemists will be working with you?'

'Just me.'

Kit, smiling, couldn't help herself.

'Then you shall get on well together.'

5

Inventing an Icon

In 1923, on his thirtieth birthday, my grandfather began work. He was given a formal tour of the factory and introduced to the senior staff before being shown to a small laboratory. It was disconcertingly empty but for a long narrow bench with a sink in the centre and a single desk.

A cigarette tin and matchbook lying on the bench told him that the previous occupant had only recently vacated. From the factory floor beyond he fancied he felt the glare of hostile looks.

Cyril was provided with a lab coat, but what he really needed, the very reason for his appointment, was a regular supply of *Saccharomyces cerevisiae* – brewer's yeast. He soon discovered that Fred Walker had already struck a deal with Carlton & United Breweries to secure a year's supply of the critical ingredient.

Cyril was armed to embark upon his mission. From what I've been able to discover, there was nothing my grandfather enjoyed more than a challenge, particularly one that might break new scientific ground. It did not seem particularly important whether the subject of his investigations was the deadly devil's porridge or the by-product of beer production. Fred Walker had hired an irrepressibly curious mind disciplined by the dangers and demands of war and Cyril applied himself with rigour to the task at hand.

But the excitement of being a pioneer was tempered by the fact that there were few who could assist him in his explorations. He chased down old university contacts and wrote to colleagues across the seas in search of clues to a process of which there was really only rudimentary knowledge.

One of the few people working in the field was a man called Frederick Hopkins who had gained the chair of biochemistry at Cambridge University at the outbreak of World War I. Hopkins was one of the only scientists Cyril knew of to enquire at length into the metabolic process of cells and Cyril pestered his English friends for their understanding of his work. Even so, the realities of seamail meant that it took months before he received any reply.

In the meantime barrels of yeast arrived by truck from Abbotsford. The stuff was pungent, brown and bitter. When the lids were lifted the reek was ghastly – a demonic concoction of rotting compost and stale eggs. Yet through some mysterious alchemy, some trick of science, Cyril was expected to transform this foul fungal mash into a flavoursome food product that Fred Walker could proudly sell to households across the nation.

Success hinged upon a detailed understanding of the autolysis of yeast. Autolysis was itself a product of the death of cells, the rupturing and breaking down of the yeast's very structure. In fact, the enzymes and proteins actually attacked each other in a sort of bizarre murder-suicide. Fred's fabulous new health product would be based on decay and decomposition. If only the housewives knew! But only an intricate knowledge of that process would unlock its secrets and deliver what Cyril's employer required.

After a few months Cyril began to make headway and the workers beyond the lab door soon developed a grudging admiration for the hardworking university man. They looked on in wonder as new and unusual equipment was delivered and installed in the laboratory. It was becoming so crowded that drums and holding vats were moved outside onto the factory floor. It was clear to everyone that there was something interesting happening behind the lab doors, but no one could quite put their finger on what it was. Only Fred and Cyril really knew what they were seeking to achieve, what the constant testing and re-testing of the smelly, glutinous brown substances was all about.

Cyril's report of Yeast Experiment 54 in August 1923 recorded his 'second attempt to debitter in centrifuge basket by simply washing, allowing ample time of contact of soda solution'. But the results remained unsatisfactory. Yeast Experiments 55 and 56 fared no better. Nothing yet resembled – or smelled or tasted like – anything that anyone would willingly eat. Still, Cyril pressed on, happily obsessed with the notion of making a silk purse from his sow's ear.

Unfortunately for my grandfather's family, his obsession was not confined to the company lab. At home he had the perfect guinea pigs to taste test his results.

'The old man was always trying stuff on us,' my father once told me, a distaste that defied the ages still curling his lip. Kit was even less enthusiastic. Cousins and friends didn't escape Cyril's trials either. My grandfather would have been unperturbed by their reactions, would have remained optimistic as ever. It was all part of the road to discovery and a few little bumps along the way weren't going to deter him.

I visited Fred Walker's factory for the first time some eighty years on from Cyril's experiments. We lined up to put on hairnets, plastic safety glasses and bright orange 'happy jackets' before being given a tour.

'It's still packed in glass, you know, not like peanut butter. You can't mess with Vegemite,' an employee proudly told me.

I was impressed by the warm reception from the workers on the factory floor. I felt a cringe of embarrassment but was delighted to discover that despite the passage of time my grandfather was still held in high regard. The Melbourne factory was high-tech, clean and modern. The head food technologist was in awe of what Cyril had been able to achieve with such limited resources and enthusiastically explained the autolysis process. She declined, however, to go into any real detail. Cyril's secrets, his hard-won formulae, were now one of the company's most treasured – and valuable – possessions. But as the corporate wings folded, my curiosity only grew.

On a later visit I met with the company librarian and was given a polite tour of the archives, where I was shown a few snippets of information and a good photo of Cyril in the lab. I was fascinated by my grandfather's story, but as with many family histories, only disparate fragments seemed to have endured. And yet, serendipity – that elusive friend of both researcher and scientist – played a large part in my unearthing a few more facts.

My cousin is a doctor with a practice in the outer Melbourne suburbs. He was collecting a patient from the waiting room one morning when he heard his partner call for his next victim: 'Keith Farrer.'

Farrer, my cousin knew, was a colleague of Cyril's at the Fred Walker Company and, later, at Kraft. As soon as travel would allow, I was in the ninety-three-year-old's kitchen listening to him talk about Cyril while my young daughter took notes. We spoke at length about all sorts of matters, though, after we left I felt I had missed an opportunity to learn more about the scientific process that Cyril had discovered. I rang and explained my deficiencies. Keith Farrer's reply came by mail a few days later:

> On reflection I realised that I had given you only the sketchiest idea of the original Vegemite process ... The science behind it is fairly simple (if you say it quickly), i.e. the proteolic enzymes of the dying / dead cells attack the cell proteins and break them down successively through the increasingly soluble proteoses, peptones and peptides to amino acids which pass through the cell walls into the surrounding liquid and carry with them the vitamins and minerals. Exactly the same thing goes on, but only very slowly, in 'hung' meat ... Cyril understood this and in the days when vitamins were only beginning to be understood he realised that this product would be a good source of the whole group of B of vitamins of which B1 was the most important.

Farrer was right. It was simple if you said it quickly. But Cyril clearly had an interest in the potential health benefits of the new product beyond a mere chemist's curiosity.

By the spring of 1923 Cyril had succeeded in developing a complex process to produce a paste of a more palatable nature. Or so he thought.

Aside from the chemist and his children, Fred Walker was one of the few people who had regularly sampled the yeast product throughout its evolutionary stages. Other workers in the factory took one look at the concoction and downright refused.

Fred tried to goad the doubters to taste by telling them that if they lived in Hong Kong it would have been considered an insult to refuse an offering of food. And he also joked that they ought to remember where their wages came from. Cyril, of course, had tasted and re-tasted his vexed creation so often that his own opinion was no longer useful.

In addition to his work on Vegemite, Cyril also had to work on fine-tuning a number of other products, including canned meats and Fred's famously temperamental potted cheese. All of which took time.

Just as the company founder started to wonder if the new yeast product would *ever* be suitable for the kitchen shelf, Cyril finally gave Fred the answer he was seeking one August evening.

It was all systems go and all that was now required was the plant and equipment.

The two men sat at Fred's desk as Cyril meticulously described the process, scrawling out a chart in pencil on butcher's paper. It was really a series of linked processes, commencing with the sieving and treatment of the yeast slurry. Then followed washes, filter pressing, boiling and separating. It concluded with concentration of the product in a vacuum pan, an apparatus through which evaporation could take place at low temperatures.

Even with Fred's knowledge of food manufacturing, certain aspects of the operation still eluded him. At a certain point on the flowchart, Fred saw that Cyril had written the initials SCP.

'Don't worry about that,' Cyril said. 'It's just lab talk for an intermediate product.'

Fred still appeared confused.

'I need to add product for flavour but I haven't got the exact amounts yet.'

There was also the small matter of holding the half-processed product at 120 degrees Fahrenheit (49°C) while stirring it for sixteen hours.

Fred challenged his chemist.

'Who's going to be here in the middle of the night to stir this stuff?'

Cyril was unfazed.

'Perhaps we can improvise with dairy equipment.'

Fred installed the required machinery and valuable factory space was given over to production of the extract. The result was a black paste that at best resembled axle grease and, at worst, tar. The distinctive smell did not make its creator popular with his factory colleagues. And still the process remained far from perfect.

One morning during testing Cyril was horrified to see what appeared to be fragments of glass poking through the surface of the extract. He initially thought it to be the result of a broken jar, but the jars used were amber in colour and these fragments were clear. He removed one with a pair of tweezers and examined it closely. He took it between his thumb and forefinger and squeezed it, but it didn't draw blood. The worker at Cyril's shoulder was alarmed to see him then raise the small splinter of glass to his lips. But the chemist had his reasons.

'It's okay, it's just sodium chloride ... you know, crystals.'

After a few days Cyril had managed to remedy the problem, but its occasional recurrence threatened to jeopardise release of the product. The newspapers were only too willing to report on curious oddities found in food products, from the bizarre to the gruesome. Nails had been found in cheese and a bullet in a can of jam. Tainted products were the bane of all food manufacturers. Even the most remote suggestion that glass, or anything like it, had been found in the Walker company's new product, particularly one which already needed to overcome beauty issues, would be fatal. Fortunately, Cyril managed to iron out the problems before any jars hit the shelves.

The hunt was then on to find a suitably attractive name, a brand that was catchy and that would profitably reflect the product's health-promoting attributes. Fred advertised a public competition through the newspapers, offering a prize of £50; not surprisingly, he received numerous entries. It was reported that he was unable to choose between them and so, on a weekend excursion to the Dandenong Ranges to Melbourne's east, he put the names into a hat and invited his daughter Sheila to draw one out.

At last in 1923 the mysterious new product rolled off the Walker factory lines. It was packed in a two-ounce amber glass jar, its shape reminiscent of a little lighthouse. And on a bright orange and red label was the name 'Vegemite'. Below that was the description 'Pure Vegetable Extract'.

Fred Walker finally felt confident to negotiate a deal with

the brewery for an ongoing supply of yeast. The sum of £500 was also set aside from the company's advertising budget to promote Vegemite over its first six months. Plans were made to erect stands at the popular Sydney and Melbourne royal agricultural shows. Vegemite was spruiked to the public as 'Nature's Wonder Food' – a product of particular benefit to children. 'Throw away the medicine bottle,' exhorted one ad, 'and replace it with a jar of Vegemite.'

The Fred Walker Company's reputation was sufficient to break down resistance from bemused grocers and storekeepers. Public acceptance, however, was a very different matter – despite Fred's best efforts, no amount of advertising would get the new product moving off the shelves. Cyril's complex chemistry may have been impressive on paper, but it appeared the result was simply too unseemly and unfamiliar to win the public's heart. After the pride of seeing the fruits of my grandfather's long hours of labour in the lab roll out through the factory doors, Fred's reports of poor sales results must have been deflating. Yet Cyril's only assistant, a boy of just sixteen who had won his job by turning up uninvited at the lab door every morning for a month, remembered a different experience.

At the time Theo Easton was studying chemistry at the Working Men's College, later to become known as the Royal Melbourne Institute of Technology. He was kept busy testing the product through all its various chemical stages and recalled that Vegemite seemed both a high company priority and a matter of personal importance to Fred Walker:

> This was a truly exciting period. Here was a new product swinging into full production. We had shifts working

around the clock producing stocks for distribution throughout the country.

But sampling and re-sampling the stuff took its toll on the young boy's tastebuds. 'Oddly enough, it's difficult to recall my first reaction to it,' Easton later reported.

As Vegemite began to roll off the lines, the demands of Cyril's work became all-consuming. My grandfather would rise at dawn to catch the first tram of the day and arrive home late. Sometimes he would get up in the middle of the night to go into the kitchen and spend an hour writing notes before returning to bed. He worked every Saturday morning and sometimes would work into the afternoon. His steely focus was to make Walker's products, particularly Vegemite, a success.

At home in Brighton, however, Kit was struggling to cope. The couple now had three children under the age of four. Kit was feeling increasingly isolated, left to raise the children and manage the household without support. During the week she had few people to talk to and it was a long couple of months' wait for replies to her letters home to Scotland.

In the winter Cyril would leave work early on a Saturday to go to a local park to play lacrosse. It was an interesting, if somewhat obscure choice of recreation. Lacrosse is considered to have been America's first national sport and is believed to have been originated by native North Americans, playing in 'teams' numbering upwards of a hundred players. Apparently they pursued each other over a field as large as several kilometres with a makeshift ball and their netted sticks. Some experts believed this served as a form of training for hunting and war, as a means of settling disputes and as an offering of thanks to the Creator.

Lacrosse was introduced in Australia in the 1870s by a Canadian with the striking name of Lambton L. Mount. Mount was moved to import forty lacrosse sticks after viewing what he considered to be the inferior spectacle of Australian Rules football. Such was lacrosse's consequent rise in popularity that an international match staged at the Melbourne Cricket Ground in 1907 attracted a crowd of over thirty thousand people. By the early 1920s, the city boasted some twenty clubs comprising a wide variety of players: university students, labourers, factory workers and businessmen alike. Despite its genteel name, lacrosse was fast, often brutal and left its players little time to dwell on the more banal problems of everyday life. For Cyril it was a useful way of relieving the pressures of work and home.

According to my father, lacrosse also resulted in the occasional injury and he told me how Cyril would return home on Saturday afternoons sometimes with bloodied brows and black eyes.

On Sundays the Callister family would walk as one to the local Presbyterian church. While Cyril considered himself the more pious, Kit enjoyed the company of the other women. As they chatted my grandfather would take his tea with the men amid a cloud of pipe smoke. One particular Sunday morning his brethren had poked fun at some lacrosse-related injury, and one of the wags even suggested that perhaps Cyril's beloved new 'wonder food' might fix the bruising and swelling. When sufficient teasing had been done their talk, as always, turned to sport.

In October 1923 sport meant horseracing and football and, more specifically, the grand final chances of the 'Same Olds' and the 'Maroons' – the Essendon and Fitzroy clubs. That year the big game had been postponed from the previous week when the MCG was flooded, meaning that it would now coincide with one of the most important Spring Carnival horseracing events, the Caulfield Cup.

Then, as now, sport was a unifying force. In uncertain economic times it offered an affordable escape from the hardships of work for those who had it and the depressing monotony of searching for employment for those who didn't. It crossed divides of class, background and religion. When the teams ran out on to the ground or the horses bolted down the track all became equal.

Beyond the sporting arena, however, unrest was growing. Five years after the cessation of war the country's torn social fabric was yet to be mended. And now the fragile underpinnings of civil order were about to be exposed for all to see.

On Saturday, 3 November, Cyril arrived at work to be greeted by a disturbing scene at the factory gates. Fred and a number of workers were milling around, makeshift weapons in hand. Cyril was unable to decipher their nervous chatter and his concerns rose upon talking with his uncharacteristically anxious employer.

The police, 'the wallopers' as the workers referred to them, had gone on strike. Poor working conditions, overstretched resources and an inept administration had pushed the lawkeepers to the limit. It was said that the officers' horses were treated better than their riders. As a result of their absence there had been rioting in the city overnight with shop windows smashed, premises looted and even trams overturned. There were rumours that people had been killed. John Monash and the army's top man, Gallipoli veteran Harry Chauvel, had been called in to raise a citizens' militia to help restore order.

Early blame was directed towards an unspecified criminal element. Fred wasn't taking any chances and organised all available male workers to protect the factory.

Cyril noted how the men immediately fell silent as their boss began to address them.

They all knew Fred well, but they could also sense that he wasn't comfortable speaking to them en masse. He was a man more given to personal interaction and he knew each and every one of them by name. His generosity and willingness to treat them as equals had won a rare respect. He gave them tea breaks when other bosses across the city gave their workers nothing but grief. He was genuinely interested in their welfare and had been proved right when he said the new chemist posed no threat. His charitable acts were near legend. All knew the story of how Fred had once arrived home in winter without his treasured cashmere coat. When his wife asked where it was he told her that he had given it to a less fortunate soul he'd come across in the street who looked cold.

Cyril was deeply unsettled to see these loyal men armed with cricket bats and timber batons fashioned from packing cases. If the looters and rioters came he knew their resolve would be unshakeable and dangerous in its intensity, particularly among those who had known active combat. Early that evening Cyril returned home to his family, leaving Fred and his workers to guard the factory. Another night of violence erupted on Melbourne's streets and just after midnight a group of men returning home to the dockside suburbs challenged the workers at the gate. As it happened, there was no need for bats or batons – the night watchman simply set the dogs on them and the would-be troublemakers ran for their lives.

By the beginning of 1924, new threats were gathering. The slow uptake of Vegemite and pressures at home were beginning to weigh my grandfather down. Fred confided in him that the general economic outlook was worsening and his major creditor was becoming anxious about the company's unusual ideas and expansive plans.

Even the neighbours were complaining. It seems the vile stench from processing vats of yeast for Vegemite production was seeping into their homes. Combined with the meat extraction fumes that flavoured the air with Bonox, it was all too much. Fearful that a bigger public stink might ensue and affect sales, the company sought novel solutions, both deodorising the wastewater from the yeast filtration process and raising the height of the factory chimney by twenty feet.

Buyers' resistance to Vegemite contined and Cyril soon found himself in conflict with Fred's head salesman over the fledgling product. Billy Shannon claimed that he was doing his best to improve sales, but try as he might, more product was now returning to the factory than was being sent out. Meanwhile, the British product Marmite was being imported in increasing quantities and promoted with heightened vigour. Sanitarium had recognised the threat and sought to kill off both Vegemite and Bonox with a deft new strategy. 'Marmite,' their advertising slogan claimed, was 'a man's drink … very economical to use … ask your wife to buy the Large Jars!'

Cyril was infuriated that Shannon, the very man who could determine Vegemite's fate, admitted to a personal distaste for it. The sales manager stood his ground. He told Cyril that they had given the product their best shot and that it might be time to pull it off the market.

After this heated exchange my grandfather stormed off in search of Fred to plead his case. His assistant Theo recalled his glum comments on returning to the laboratory.

'You and I could be looking for a job next week.'

When Walker eventually got wind of this dispute, he tried to reassure Cyril, though even he appeared to be looking for ways to move on from the Vegemite debacle and bolster his shaky creditor's confidence.

He told Cyril that he had negotiated for new meat product lines – lunchette and ham pate – from a Tasmanian cold storage company. My grandfather's spirits fell. It was difficult to see how he could put his expertise and innovative skills to much use in packaging processed meats. But there remained one other possibility.

As Vegemite struggled to find support, Cyril had been continuing his research into one of Fred's other pet loves – cheese. He had contacted research colleagues and dairy producers across the country, and had corresponded with Edward William Coon (the man who patented a method of fast maturation of cheese via high temperature and humidity) in the US. He had waded through reams of material but only now felt that he was making some real progress.

In an effort to avert a future slaving away over cold meats, Cyril worked hard to secure Fred's backing. His lab work had achieved some promising results with emulsifiers such as sodium phosphate and he told his boss the company should continue to work on producing a cheese that wouldn't spoil. Emulsifiers, a kind of chemical glue that prevented cheese from separating into a fatty slop when heated, also had the effect of prolonging its shelf life. Buoyed by this report, Fred was happy to let his chemist pursue his investigations while he consolidated the Tasmanian meat-processing deal.

Cyril made rapid progress and learned that by adding the right amount of emulsifier the cheese would melt to an appetising texture. But he still struggled to achieve consistent results to create a foolproof formula that would satisfy the increasingly demanding consumer. As the application of technology to food accelerated, bringing new and improved products to the corner store, so customers' expectations had grown.

As luck would have it, developments overseas were conspiring in Cyril and Fred's favour. Electricity had modernised not just the workplace but also the domestic kitchen. In 1919, Charles P. Strite, a mechanic from Minnesota in the US, patented a novel device to grill bread. With the inclusion of springs and a variable timing mechanism, the pop-up toaster was born. Now versions of the appliance were starting to appear in Australia, though it would be a few years yet before the invention of its convenient cousin – sliced bread.

Electric stoves were also beginning to be installed in the kitchens of wealthier homes along with time- and labour-saving devices such as the popular American Sunbeam Mixmasters. Poorer homes, however, had neither the inventions nor the electricity to power them.

By the middle of 1924 Fred had made good with his acquisition of the rights to 'Lunchette' and 'Ham Pate'. He also negotiated for plant and equipment and set the business up in premises leased from the Dandenong Bacon Company. Two other new products were introduced – 'Camp Pie' (an unsightly yet popular concoction of offal and fat) and a pork brawn. To his relief, Cyril was left to explore the mysteries of processed cheese while a Mr Shand was brought across Bass Strait to start up the meat processing operation. But it was only weeks before Shand suddenly quit his post without notice.

Lacking a ready replacement, Fred sent Cyril over to get the plant operational. The only joy my grandfather found in his relocation was the opportunity to don his leather jacket and ride his new Douglas motorcycle out to the factory each morning.

Meat canning was a noisy, smelly business that still involved a number of practices inherited from the previous century. On one occasion a fatigued worker left a batch boiling too long in the hot oil and cans began to burst towards the ceiling, causing a panic. The Dandenong plant produced nearly three thousand cans of processed meat per day. Some lunchtimes Cyril would challenge a co-worker to a canning contest, the winner being the man who could turn out the greatest number using hand-operated crimpers.

Meat preservation had received a boost in Australia in the 1860s when a viral cattle disease called rinderpest reached plague proportions in England and triggered a marked demand for Australian canned meat.

It was early 1925 before Cyril was finally relieved of his position and replaced by another chemist. Once back in his South Melbourne lab, he came to the sudden realisation that the cheese problem he had still to solve was not unlike that he had initially faced with Vegemite. The only success he was having in developing cheese with any real consistency was through applying a process he had obtained from one of his fellow researchers overseas. That method was, however, secured by a watertight patent in the US.

Cyril discussed his dilemma with Fred and within a few months his employer had set sail with his wife and daughter for California. The letter of introduction he carried was to a cheesemaker of high repute, a Canadian by the name of James L. Kraft.

The Big Cheese

Across a sea of time, the young James Kraft trailed along behind a draughthorse, watching as the old plough it hauled carved a furrow through the Ontario prairie. Every few hundred yards he would drop the worn reins from his hands to bend down and quickly work through the loosened soil. As the horse slowly drew away, he would feel out his prize. If he was lucky the ground would offer up an Indian arrowhead or other such native artefact. This he would hold up very close to his eyes, squinting in admiration. Squinting because he was almost blind.

One summer day on the northern shores of Lake Erie, a chance occurrence cleared the fog from the boy's future. A passer-through engaged Kraft to groom his horse and wash his buggy. As Kraft set about the task the man watched him with intense interest. When the boy had finished, the traveller asked him to look into his eyes. He held his gaze for a moment and then smiled.

'You're going over to Buffalo tomorrow and get fitted for a pair of spectacles!'

Kraft laughed and told the man that with ten brothers and sisters there was no money for glasses. But the eye doctor simply smiled back, reached into a valise and handed over a pair for the boy to try. The story later appeared in Kraft's memoirs, where he wrote: 'I cannot think of another act of human kindness during my lifetime which can compare with his.'

Kraft's journey to commercial prosperity began in the early 1890s with a lowly paid job in a grocery store in Fort Erie, just south of Niagara Falls. It was his entrée to the world of food and commerce. When he had saved a small sum of money he invested in a cheese company a few kilometres over the American border in Buffalo, New York State, and by the turn of the century had made the move to Chicago.

Kraft's ascent of the corporate ladder was cut short by unscrupulous business partners, leaving him little money and few options. He could not contemplate a return to farming and so invested his last remaining capital in a horse and wagon. Rising in the hours before dawn, he would load a cargo of cheeses and deliver it to markets and merchants across the city. Over the next five years business steadily grew. By 1909, four of his siblings had joined him and the company of J. L. Kraft & Bros was born.

Kraft wanted to produce a cheese that wouldn't spoil so quickly in the summer months and could be transported long distances. By the beginning of World War I, he had established a cheese manufacturing plant in Stockton, California, and was distributing more than thirty varieties across the country. During the war the company supplied six million pounds (more than 2700 tonnes) of a specially prepared pasteurised cheese that could survive a lengthy journey at sea and still be edible by troops on arrival. Legend had it that the company founder had stumbled upon the formula himself, experimenting in his own kitchen with an old copper kettle and double boiler.

In 1916, when Kraft was granted a patent, jealous competitors proclaimed that he was 'murdering the cheese' and that his creation bore no resemblance to the traditional product. The critics were, however, quickly silenced by the cheese's success in the marketplace and other cheese companies rushed to experiment with similar processes, and with equally encouraging results. The Phenix Cheese Company of New York created Philadelphia Cream Cheese, a brand synonymous with one of America's favourite treats, cheesecake. But Phenix was too late to file its patent and would later join forces with Kraft. Other companies followed suit and through acquisition and expansion Kraft became a major producer on several continents. At home in the United States they were now manufacturing an astonishing forty per cent of all cheese sold and consumed.

One morning in October 1924 James Kraft's secretary announced that there was an Austrian waiting to see him.

'I think you mean Australian,' he corrected.

Fred Walker and James Kraft quickly developed a rapport. On being given a tour of the Stockton factory, Walker realised that every product development idea he had ever contemplated was already rolling out of this enormous operation in such volume that it was near impossible to comprehend. They were men of the same water, only one was a minnow.

They discussed Kraft's patented cheese process in detail and James was impressed with Fred's knowledge. Fred explained that his chemist Cyril Callister had been exploring the process in Melbourne but soon realised that a patent had already been filed.

The men's conversation roamed across every area of modern industry from labour management to time and motion studies. The development of efficient means for the mass production of goods had been advancing steadily since the introduction of the Ford Motor Company's moving assembly line in 1913. That process had been inspired by the overhead rail and trolley system employed to move meat along the butchering line in Chicago slaughterhouses. Kraft was applying many of these same principles to his cheese production and canning processes.

Fred knew that numerous American companies had set up back home and were now importing and implementing similar practices, and that to compete he would need to modernise his operations. In addition, both men were well aware of the intrinsic value of a lean and efficient workforce. Fred listened intently as his host spoke of his management theories, vastly more scientific than his own more instinctive style.

James Kraft was also taking the advertising of his products to new levels. Literally. He boasted to Fred of his 'signs in the sky' – a series of billboards adorning Chicago's elevated train network – and of his ambition to see the name Kraft on the side of 'any moving conveyance'. But in spite of such great modern developments he was also at pains to stress the importance of maintaining direct contact with customers, explaining how his business had initially grown by mailing circulars to grocers he supplied and others he didn't. Despite the substantial demands that success had since wrought, the company founder still made time to call on some clients in person.

Fred was impressed both by Kraft's vision and achievements. When he arrived back at the plush Palmer House Hotel in Chicago he corralled the bellhop and gave him an urgent message to cable, accompanied by a generous tip. Back at the South Melbourne factory the following morning Cyril was handed a slip of yellow paper that read: 'Cyril – have Kraft patent prepare necessary arrangements Fred.'

Cyril was elated. Finally they had the capacity to deliver a cheese product that would travel, keep and stand alone in the marketplace. The only other decent Australian cheeses didn't travel far beyond the farmhouse door. Cyril's research had identified the failure of the cheese starters as the major challenge in producing a reliable product.

Further, his work on Vegemite had given him an insight into the relatively new science of microbiology and the concept of food production as a technology. Now with the Kraft patent secured and an air of confidence permeating the company, he scaled up his laboratory operations to permit deeper investigations.

Elsewhere in Australia, others were pursuing similar paths. In April 1926, the commitment of Prime Minister Stanley Bruce to foster scientific investigation saw the founding of the Council for Scientific and Industrial Research – later to become the CSIRO. In the organisation's first year, forty-one scientists worked from premises rented from a technical college in the inner-Melbourne suburb of Brunswick before moving to the new national capital of Canberra. One of its three executive members was Cyril's university lecturer Professor David Rivett, who had also worked in munitions research in Swindon. Rivett's fellow members were the inventor of the racecourse totalisator machine, George Julius, and electrical engineer William Newbigin. Ormie Masson was appointed head of the CSIR's Victorian State Committee. The organisation was given £250,000, which was anticipated to fund investigations for several years. Among the five topics listed for immediate study by the council's experts and researchers was the preservation of foodstuffs.

Research would focus on improving the durability of milk and butter, and finding ways of overcoming rots in eggs and fruits that were cold preserved to meet out-of-season demand. Some problems that were directed to CSIR, however, had eccentric and super-specific origins. Outbound passenger liners needed a higher quality of milk that would keep for longer. And workers' discontent at the long hours involved in baking bread led to demand for a fast-rising dough.

Although Walker Company products, with the conspicuous exception of Vegemite, were performing reasonably, Fred could see more struggles ahead and, thinking of the long term, found a solution to prospective difficulties.

In May 1926, following another expedition to Chicago, the Kraft Walker Cheese Company was born. The *Argus* newspaper reported that the huge American concern had contributed to a dramatic escalation in cheese consumption in the US. Kraft was not only dominating the market but driving new demand at unprecedented speed:

The Kraft Company of America claims that by reason largely of its extensive organisation and advertising, it has aided materially in increasing the yearly consumption of cheese in the United States from about two and three quarter pounds per head of population to about four pounds a head [nearly 2 kg] within the last few years. That means an increase of about 150,000,000 pounds a year in the consumption of cheese in the United States.

These astonishing statistics were reflected by balance sheets that boasted turnover in 1925 of US$32 million. The partnership with the Fred Walker Company and subsequent manufacturing expansion in Australia promised to be a boon for employment and the dairy industry. The Kraft company story, the *Argus* said, was 'one of the romances of business of which America provides numerous examples'.

Some of those other examples were also planting their flags on Australian soil and fast becoming household names. The cereal giant Kelloggs had been producing corn flakes out of a rented premises in Chippendale in Sydney for nearly two years. Forty thousand tennis racquets and countless balls had rolled off Spalding's Melbourne production lines in 1925, the company's first year of Australian operation. British chocolate maker Cadbury had set up near Hobart with a manufacturing headquarters that included an entire village and sporting facilities. The primary motivation of these economic imperialists was to avoid high tariffs and jump the protectionist barrier that discriminated against foreign companies. Customers flocked to buy the goods they had read about in English magazines and seen in American films. General Motors was producing Chevrolets at assembly plants in five states, and Australia's first Model T Ford was being built on a makeshift production line in a disused woolshed outside Geelong. The motor car was becoming more common on city streets and Cyril steadily put aside savings in the hope of purchasing his own. With the Kraft deal a reality and prosperity seemingly assured, Fred had already ordered himself a luxurious vehicle from the Stutz motor company of Indianapolis.

During the 1920s, my grandparents occasionally attended dances and movies but for Kit the most anticipated event was the visit to Melbourne of the celebrated Russian prima ballerina Anna Pavlova. As a young girl, Kit had gone with her aspiring actress sister Leena to shows in London's West End. Some had been quite lavish, but the performance by Pavlova and her ensemble in Melbourne was, according to reports, sublime – her dying swan the pinnacle of emotional art. As the show wore on, however, my grandfather's enthusiasm waned. He counted the costume changes before moving on to a detailed study of the theatre's ceiling. Small wonder then that Kit expressed her surprise to hear Cyril give a lengthy description of the performance to an excited neighbour a few days later.

Usually Kit's social outings were limited to accompanying Cyril to professional functions, nearly always chemistry-related. The men's conversation was technical and dull and the rather snooty women who were at these events seemed dedicated to cataloguing the fruits of their husbands' success.

My grandparents didn't have a holiday house at the fashionable seaside towns of Mount Eliza or Portsea, and Kit hadn't completed her schooling at a private educational institution for ladies but at an elementary school in Annan. Although she made the most of her lot and tried to fit in, Kit was never truly comfortable with the privileged elite or those aspiring to its membership. The only times she truly seemed to relax was when she spoke of home with her friend Agnes. It seemed an age since they had conspired together to marry their Australian scientists. Kit saw Agnes as much as she could and so their children also became friends. In a further effort to combat feeling lonely, she began to take the children to her sister Hope's farm outside Shepparton more frequently, and for longer visits. There, they received the undivided attention of a couple whose own efforts at a family had been thwarted by a series of miscarriages.

Fred Walker arrived back in Australia from the US around the same time as his new car was being unloaded onto the Port Melbourne dock. The new Stutz was a head-turner, modern and powerful, much larger than the popular Model T, more a limousine than a family car. Cyril had only just purchased his 'jalopy' (as Fred referred to it) but already dreamed of something bigger and better. They weren't the only ones who had their sights on travelling the streets in style.

Joseph Leslie Taylor was born in Brighton, in Melbourne's south-east, where my grandfather now lived, in 1888 and by the age of sixteen had already earned his first conviction for insulting behaviour. A series of increasingly serious misdemeanours followed and by age twenty-five the diminutive lout with the smart mouth and squinty gaze had graduated to his first murder charge. By the time he 'borrowed' Fred Walker's new

Stutz without asking he had successfully evaded conviction on three such charges, committed innumerable other offences and become a crime lord of such notoriety that the entire city knew him simply as 'Squizzy'. He was as famous as Ned Kelly but, unlike the folk hero, few ever imagined that Taylor's motivation was anything but greed and self-aggrandisement.

Squizzy had an irrepressible penchant for publicity, writing letters and verse to newspapers while in hiding and even co-starring with his girlfriend in a movie that was later banned by the Victorian censor. When not in jail or on the run the loudly dressed criminal swaggered about the city's streets, theatres and racecourses, drawing the attention of the social elite. Perhaps it was this that prompted him to select a high profile business-man as his latest victim.

Fred Walker's grandson recalled that the first thing Fred knew about his missing Stutz was when he received a telephone call from the gangster at his South Melbourne office. Squizzy told him that he had needed the car for an errand and had taken it to St Kilda, where Walker could now pick it up at his convenience.

Fred told Taylor that he would do no such thing and politely asked that the vehicle be returned to his factory immediately. He assured him that if this request was expedited, he would refrain from contacting the police. Squizzy promptly returned the Stutz and Fred – being a man of his word but no fool – waited until he had left the premises before calling the constabulary.

While Fred and Cyril were distracted by cars, the company accountant Edward Nixon was busy putting red ink through many of Fred's more ambitious ideas. He addressed Fred and the board on essential product and strict business practice. Fred managed to wangle a few concessions but Nixon was insistent that the company had to stabilise its profit base. He had tried the new American style cheese, understood its value and was keen to get it and the new Kraft Walker 'to market' as soon as possible. Somewhat surprisingly, Nixon had also tried Vegemite:

> It's an odd thing but I don't mind it. Our sales staff take a somewhat different view and to be honest are sceptical of any health benefits or for that matter a future ...

When Fred spoke to my grandfather in his office, though, he wasn't nearly as conciliatory. The bank may have saved the company but the entrepreneur wasn't ready to be told what to do by an *accountant*! Within days, Fred formulated a plan to accelerate production of the new cheese using Kraft funds and to make it the backbone of the business. Fred handed Cyril a batch of scientific papers he'd brought from Chicago and told his bemused chemist that Kraft would be sending out one of their key men to teach the Australians the art of processed cheese.

Pioneers, Pigeons and Parwill

In early spring of 1926, Kraft Walker's head salesman, Billy Shannon, reported that sales of the new cheese packaged in a bright blue cardboard box were growing at a very healthy £100,000 per month. It was far beyond the wildest expectations and, with processing plants still being built, the company had not yet entered full production. Some other products, like canned soup, had enjoyed a good winter and figures for the traditional Red Feather potted cheese, Camp Pie and meat pastes remained steady. There were smiles around the boardroom table, but Shannon's summary was notable for its omission of any mention of Vegemite.

In truth, there was little by way of sales to report. The product had failed to capture the interest of the market and their competitor's scaled up importation and promotion of the more familiar Marmite seemed sufficient to deter customers from bothering to sample the homegrown extract. To combat this a new slogan had been tested – 'The health food with the tantalising taste' – but it appeared to have had little effect.

But the slogan wasn't mere puff. Cyril had now received research results he had been waiting on from England. Robert Plimmer, professor of chemistry and chair of the St Thomas Medical School at the University of London, had tested the extract for vitamin content and reported favourably. To the intrigue of his colleagues, Plimmer maintained a poultry farm on the flat roof of his department, which as well as supplying laboratory animals for research was known also to provide the occasional meal for his students!

In the course of testing Vegemite, Plimmer discovered that in the right dosage the extract could cure pigeons paralysed by polyneuritis – the equivalent of beriberi in humans. (Beriberi may affect the cardiovascular and nervous systems and can cause congestive heart failure.) The experiment Plimmer used had been first devised by Casimir Funk to solve the mystery of why people in East Asia who ate polished rice as a staple part of their diet developed the disease while those who ate unpolished rice did not. His findings led directly to the identification and naming of vitamins as an important element of nutrition. Plimmer wrote to Cyril and informed him that Vegemite was proven to be a reliable source of vitamin B, specifically B1 or thiamine. He added that Cyril could promote the fact that Vegemite compared favourably with other extracts, but asked that for professional reasons his name not be mentioned in any advertisement.

When Cyril told Fred of these results, the boss became more convinced than ever that the problem they were saddled with lay not with the product but with getting the public to try it. After consulting with his advertising agency Fred brought a surprising new strategy to the table to improve sales. The agency had come up with a slogan that would directly take on the competitor product and he thought it worth a try. There was only one small thing – it meant changing Vegemite's name. And the new name would be Parwill.

'Marmite but Parwill', the agency slogan ran.

It must have been interesting to see the faces and hear the debate around the boardroom table when Fred revealed his brilliant new ploy. Marmite what? Parwill what? Ma might not like it, but Pa will?

There was more than a little resistance to this new strategy. My grandfather, while sympathetic to the state of sales, considered Fred to have – putting it mildly – misjudged the public. For him the new name seemed corny and forced.

Regardless, in September 1926 jars bearing the new brand name were sent to market and tested in less populated territories. Parwill was sold in Queensland, Western Australia, South Australia, Tasmania and outback New South Wales while Vegemite remained on the shelves in the bigger east coast cities. To tempt customers into taking a chance on the 'new' extract, some larger stores offered packs of the breakfast wafers Vita-Brits free with every purchase. Yet grocers also continued to advertise their remaining stocks of the Vegemite branded jars, which must have caused a good deal of confusion.

At the same time a new promotional push for Vegemite commenced in Sydney, offering prospective customers an 'opportunity extraordinary' to win a fancy new English car, the Jowett, simply by sending in a newspaper coupon. The car itself was put on display at a Sydney showroom. The ad also offered the great unconverted masses a chance to buy, postage free, a sample jar of Vegemite at a discounted price. Despite all this effort sales remained sluggish and, if it weren't for the runaway success of the American cheese, Vegemite and Parwill might both have been pulled from the shelves for good.

Meanwhile, life at home for my grandfather was becoming increasingly complicated. The strain of raising three children was beginning to affect Kit's health and the local doctor was a frequent visitor to the house.

When Cyril found time away from the factory there were the usual family excursions, but a few Sunday hours spent frolicking on the bay's edge, fishing for yabbies at Landcox Park in Brighton East, or riding the new and absurdly high Big Dipper rollercoaster at Luna Park did little to lighten Kit's burdens. The doctor informed Cyril that her breathing problems, whether the result of neurosis or illness, were becoming serious and that she may need some help around the home.

Cyril took his family responsibilities seriously but his professional obligations could not be ignored. What was more, he had only recently begun to attend evening microbiology lectures at the University of Melbourne. This was to increase his knowledge of a field that was becoming ever more critical to the Kraft Walker company's ambitions, but it meant less and less time at home to care for Kit and the children.

In an effort to combat this, Cyril arranged for his wife's sister to come down from Shepparton. Upon observing Kit's state, Hope immediately arranged to take the children back to the bush with her. My father couldn't remember exactly how long they were separated from their mother and home, but the stay was long enough for them to attend the local school.

At the University of Melbourne, Cyril enjoyed the tutelage of William Young, a professor in biological chemistry. The academic was delighted to have such an experienced chemist among his students, and suggested to Cyril that his work on Vegemite might form the basis for a thesis and the eventual attainment of a PhD. The idea of becoming a doctor flattered Cyril, but he had another motive for returning to university: the research workload in the lab was escalating and he hoped to identify a few eager types among Young's students willing to consider a career with Kraft Walker.

Someone he had his eye on was a young woman who had grown up on the university campus, the daughter of a chemistry professor who had taught Cyril at undergraduate level. Audrey Osborne was luminously bright and had an easy confidence, possibly the result of being surrounded by academics from the time she could walk. Her mother was a gifted scientist who had taken up a career in dietetics and both parents had instilled in their daughter an interest in nutrition from an early age. Her father even gave public lectures on the necessity of healthy eating. Within the family there had never been any distinctions made on the grounds of gender and Audrey Osborne had an advanced sense of her capacity to equal, or better, any man in her chosen field. Audrey's family also had a semi-rural retreat at Warrandyte on the banks of the Yarra River and her affection for country life had led her to a degree in agriculture from which she was soon to graduate. She would be the first woman in the history of the university to do so.

This precocious young woman from Professor's Row was, as far as Cyril was concerned, just what the doctor ordered. There was, however, a problem. Audrey had already been offered a job. Her six years of study had been aided by a studentship from Victoria's Department of Agriculture and they were now keen to realise the return on their investment. Audrey, though, wasn't the type simply to do what was expected of her. By her observation, women were only given desk jobs and she wanted something 'a bit more exciting'.

Cyril swooped and, as soon as the ink was dry on her degree, Audrey Osborne took up her position as a microbiologist and food analyst at Kraft Walker.

Cyril's laboratory was fast becoming one of the country's foremost centres for food research. He employed eight scientists and assistants with backgrounds in a range of fields and regularly spoke with CSIR head Rivett at state meetings of the Chemical Institute. Rivett assured my grandfather that the organisation enjoyed the full support of Prime Minister Stanley Bruce, who was keen to nurture a progressive environment where science and industry worked for the country's mutual benefit.

On the other hand, Rivett said, Bruce's affection for the mother country seemed to frustrate other trading relationships. He also noted that Bruce didn't appear to have had any success in resolving industrial disputes. The Australian Council for Trade Unions (ACTU), founded in 1927, was taking a combative approach to improving working conditions across a large number of industries and rifts were splitting open across the nation. Bruce's Nationalist Party was actively fostering the importation of immigrant workers to boost Australian agricultural production and wages were beginning to fall.

A forty-four hour week had been achieved but rural hardships, particularly among soldier settlers like Cyril's brother-in-law Jack, were the catalyst for a population drift back to the cities, swelling unemployment and adding to wage decline. A water-side workers' strike that began in August 1928 and remained unresolved halfway through the following year triggered riots in Melbourne and ended up paralysing the ports. In retaliation the government attempted to dismantle the accepted system of wage arbitration – and its failure would also be Bruce's downfall.

Kraft Walker, with its large workforce and heavy reliance on agricultural production, was not immune to the problems besetting the nation. Like Fred, my grandfather was politically conservative and didn't have a great deal of time for the union movement, believing that workers' interests were best served by the voluntary benevolence of owners and employers.

Fred and Cyril went out of their way to champion their staff's rights and were pragmatic in their assessments. Their philosophy was simple – work with us to achieve our goals and we'll treat you well, or step out of the way and let someone else do the job. But beyond their control, beyond the Kraft Walker factory walls and beyond Australia's shores, a new storm was gathering. The world's largest industrialised economies were beginning to falter, teetering on the brink of some as yet dim and unknown future.

On Christmas Eve 1928, my grandparents drove to Shepparton to collect their children. Although they were excited to see their parents they were also sad to leave the farm. They told story after story – of swimming in the racing currents of newly carved irrigation channels, encountering huge snakes, riding out on horseback to neighbouring properties and camping under the stars.

Their uncle Jack had regaled them with tales of his travels both true and imaginary – at sea, of whales and albatrosses, and during the war, of deserts and camels – without ever mentioning a single drop of blood was spilled. With an equal mixture of fact and fiction, Auntie Hope told them about growing up with their mother, of their naughty childhood escapades in a country and time a world away.

One day near the end of their stay the children heard in the distance a low drone that gradually grew louder. They all peered skyward and there, flicking glints of sunlight into their eyes, was an aeroplane! Uncle Jack had promised one and his neighbour had made good. He made it even better by dipping a wing over the chimney top and landing in the cleared paddock just beyond the house. Jean refused to go near the contraption but Ian immediately ran over, clambered up onto the bottom wing and crawled to the open cockpit before the propeller had ceased spinning. Jack's neighbour called my father over and with the two boys harnessed in and helmeted – and a joke about hanging on tight if he flew the crate upside down – prepared to take off again.

The biplane bumped over tussocks then abruptly left the ground, crabbing sideways into the breeze. As they climbed higher it became cool, then cold. Most of the time they couldn't see a thing but when the plane banked the whole world spread out below. My uncle Ian, at only five years of age, was scared, thrilled and totally, irreversibly hooked.

It took a little over a year for Fred Walker reluctantly to concede that the Parwill rebranding exercise had failed and the decision was taken to remove the jars from sale. According to Shannon's salesmen, Kraft cheese was walking out the door but the black stuff was resolutely remaining on the shelves. The company was surviving the general downturn by parlaying profits back into promotion and developing new products to expand their territory inside the corner store.

There was no doubting their audacity. The popularity of Kraft cheese and Fred Walker's determination to promote the healthy nature of everything his company produced were the inspiration behind 'Kraftease Pills'. These weren't pills at all but tiny production line off-cuts of processed cheese rolled into a pill-like shape. The resourcefulness of squeezing every last ounce of profit from the production process was only matched by the creativity of the advertising.

The properties of Kraftease Pills, according to the *CheeseKraft* newsletter the company distributed to its retailers, were even more remarkable than Bonox. The cheesy cure-alls would, it was claimed, eradicate common ailments including influenza, indigestion, headache, acne and the curious Pain-in-the-Finger (the result perhaps of rolling little pieces of cheese into pellets?).

But that wasn't all. Showing a talent for humour, the copywriter suggested that the pills would alleviate drunkenness, unemployment, love sickness, communism and flat feet. A picture of female Kraft employees at work was even accompanied by the hilarious caption:

> No less than 50 Australian girls are engaged busily rolling
> pills of Kraftease … Girls with small thumbs roll one-

gram pills and girls with big thumbs are used for rolling two-gram pills.

It was all a lark, but Shannon's team was also geeing up shop-keepers with astonishing true stories from across the globe. The processed cheese had been successfully shipped to India, Malaya and Africa without refrigeration. Whether there was actually a market in these destinations was beside the point – Kraft cheese remained palatable no matter how far afield it travelled.

One story from America emerged that a block of cheese had been found untouched by human hand after a decade. When the trusty tinfoil wrapper had been removed, inspection revealed it to be as edible and unspoiled as the day it was made. Sir Douglas Mawson was so impressed with its durability he took the indestructible cheese with him on the British, Australian and New Zealand Antarctic Mission in 1929. Unlike its poor cousin, Vegemite, Kraft cheese was already inspiring the folk legends that attended an icon. More importantly – and even less like Vegemite – it was becoming a household staple no family could live without.

The Wider World

In the winter of 1929, after a two-day train trip, Cyril walked into the lip-cracking wind blowing across Brisbane's George Street and arrived at the doors of the Supreme Court of Queensland. Unfortunately there was no time for a brief stop in Sydney to visit Reg.

Cyril lugged an attaché case bursting with technical and legal documents. He had been well briefed and felt adequately prepared but he resented being there at all. If not for the avaricious behaviour of one of the company's young assistant engineers he would have been happily testing some compound or other back at his familiar lab bench.

Frank Heinecke had always been an enthusiastic employee, in retrospect perhaps excessively so, often pestering Cyril with questions, not all of which seemed relevant to the job at hand. It wasn't entirely unusual. Kraft Walker nurtured a culture of enquiry and encouraged its staff to broaden their understanding of the company's operations. With all his staff, Cyril tried to be patient and explain the scientific processes in language as simple as he could muster. The company believed that eagerness was a superior guide to future success than qualifications, and it was also easier to train a keen novice.

It wasn't the young man's curiosity that had first raised suspicions, though. He had been observed hovering over the loaf-filling machine and pasteurisation vats, notebook in hand a number of times. His excuses when challenged and the growing frequency of these incidents were what prompted Cyril to speak with the head engineer.

Then one day Heinecke was suddenly gone, an ailing mother in Sydney purportedly requiring his immediate attention. He returned some days later, but was no sooner back than off again. Upon his eventual return his conduct and demeanour were deemed unsatisfactory and he was fired.

The Supreme Court heard that the man proceeded directly to Brisbane. He met with a Kenneth McAnulty in Stanley Street, South Brisbane, just a few hundred yards from the Woollongabba cricket ground. But the two didn't have sport in mind. Instead McAnulty was provided with the final instalment of the closely guarded and patented Kraft cheese making process.

Within months Kraft Walker had a serious rival. Maxam cheese was packaged in a yellow and green box and marketed in almost identical fashion. In March 1928 an advertorial was placed in Brisbane's *Courier* newspaper spruiking the new product:

In yesterday's 'Courier' an announcement was made regarding the introduction to Queensland housewives of a new Queensland-made pasteurised cheese, known as 'Maxam' cheese, and featuring 'The Maxam Maid' as a trademark. It has been recognised for some time that if a pasteurised cheese of this type were made in the State it would be ideally suited to local climatic conditions. Maxam cheese is sold in new triangle cartons of 8oz and in triangle 5lb blocks, cut to any desired weight. It is neatly wrapped in two-colour tinfoil, and protected from the carton and box by greaseproof paper. It is a mild, matured cheese, and will keep indefinitely if the foil is not removed. Although only placed before the Public yesterday, a 'big demand has resulted' and the public show every evidence of preferring this new 'Maxam' cheese, which is destined to became a big industry in this State.

A travelling Kraft Walker salesman alerted his bosses and Cyril and Fred were both furious. While there was little they could do to pursue their former employee, litigation was instantly commenced against McAnulty for breach of patent.

The barrister engaged was a man familiar to Cyril, as he was to most of the nation's business fraternity. But Cyril had a deeper connection. Since their days at Grenville College in Ballarat, Robert 'Dag' Menzies had made a spectacular rise to political and legal fame. He had been elected to the Victorian Legislative Assembly and recently made a name for himself by attempting to stymie the prime minister's push to grant the Commonwealth additional powers at the expense of the states.

Menzies enjoyed Cyril's tale of industrial espionage but

advised him that the case would likely hinge on the wording of the original US patent. Cyril endured two days of legal bickering before finally taking the oath. The next morning an account of his testimony ran in the *Courier* under the headline 'Devastating Eloquence':

> Evidence given by a technical expert in a Supreme Court action yesterday savoured more of a professional address to students than a recital of cold facts. The question at issue had to do with cheese and surrounded by dozens of packets of the delectable product the 'Professor' with painstaking care gave an elaborate disquisition upon the blending of cheeses, the encouragement or discouragement of bacteria, the process of manufacture ... Counsel was held spellbound by academic eloquence.

The *CheeseKraft* newsletter reported that when an officer of the court finally dared interrupt Cyril, the chemist was reminded 'that even shorthand wizards have their limitations'. The article noted that the stenographer registered relief and 'stroked his aching right wrist'.

Many in the court were fascinated to hear the scientific description of a product more usually taken for granted. Justice Henchman described cheddar cheese as 'an emulsion of fat in a gel of casein and water' and suggested that 'the seriously curious might want to read the judgment to find out how emulsifiers were used to get the desired plastic homogenous glossy mass'. This, of course, wasn't how Kraft wanted their most popular product represented to the public.

When McAnulty took the stand, he told the court that he had

obtained all of his information from Frank Ernest Heinecke, who was employed by Kraft at the time. Further details then emerged of how the patented process was smuggled out of the Kraft Walker factory in Melbourne:

> Frank Ernest Heinecke gave evidence that he had been in the employment of the Kraft Walker Cheese Co. Pty. Ltd. before it started to manufacture cheese in 1926 ... He first met defendant in Melbourne in July 1927. McAnulty told Heinecke that he was a cheese manufacturer in Queensland, and that he was determined at all costs to make processed cheese after the Kraft style. He offered Heinecke a position, but he declined to have anything to do with the proposal. McAnulty persisted, and eventually Heinecke said that he would probably go to Queensland. McAnulty offered Heinecke two £10 notes for his expenses, but he said that he did not want them.

Heinecke told the court that he had met McAnulty at Toowoomba, west of Brisbane, towards the end of September 1927. They drove to the defendant's factory, about ten miles (sixteen kilometres) from Toowoomba, and there he was shown details of McAnulty's business dealings. McAnulty told him that he was determined, at all costs, to 'have a go at this process cheese'. Later McAnulty said that he had been experimenting for a considerable time with unsatisfactory results and, before leaving Toowoomba, Heinecke gave McAnulty a rough sketch of a kettle similar to that used in the Kraft Walker factory. Despite this, McAnulty had difficulty replicating the process and told Heinecke via telephone that he was having trouble with the 'filling and texture' of the cheese. He pleaded with Heinecke to return to Queensland to assist him: 'At the urgent request of defendant, witness agreed to come to Queensland in March 1928.'

McAnulty again met Heinecke at Toowoomba, and this time they travelled together by train to Ipswich. Heinecke then stayed about ten days in Brisbane. At the Maxam factory he manufactured some cheese for McAnulty similar to that made at the Kraft factory.

It took several months before Justice Henchman brought down his judgment in favour of Kraft, by which time Cyril was back in Melbourne. No one had been in a hurry to bring arguments to a conclusion. With success seemingly on their side there was also no one on the Kraft Walker board who begrudged the expense – it was far less than the damage that might have ensued from suffering a competitor in the marketplace. A few days later, however, the solicitors informed Cyril that an appeal against Justice Henchman's judgment had been lodged with the High Court in Melbourne.

On 24 October 1929, the world's most powerful economy imploded. The Wall Street stock market crashed and the ensuing days and weeks saw global financial markets collapse. It was swift and devastating. Australia's export trade in wool and wheat, already in decline, nosedived. Funds dried up and for those out of work, money and self-respect evaporated.

Unemployment lines rapidly swelled and the worst was yet to come. Even before the crash unemployment rates had been well above ten per cent as the country struggled to adjust to the postwar world. One returned soldier later lamented that he had spent the whole period from one war to the next travelling the country looking for work. He was not alone and now many thousands more would join him. Desperation for work sent hordes of men knocking at every factory door. Eventually a sign was erected at the Kraft Walker gates that read, 'Sorry, we regret no jobs'.

Cyril's own job was, for the moment, secure. But less fortunate friends and relatives began to call at his home, cap in hand. Cyril and Kit obliged where they could, assisting with money for necessities. Meanwhile his company's fortunes still hung in the balance, swinging on the High Court's decision as to whether a competitor could be allowed to flood the market with a copycat cheese made from an illicitly obtained recipe.

Shortly before Christmas, five High Court judges sat to hear the legal argument. Representing McAnulty was Reginald Bonney, a distinguished King's Counsel from Sydney and a renowned patent specialist. Opposing him was the distinguished King's Counsel and politically ascendant Robert Menzies. The case had been set down to be heard over four days.

At the end of each day's proceedings, my grandfather badgered Menzies as to the likelihood of success. The experienced barrister gave little away but on the fourth and final day he indicated that it was going to be close. In his opinion, the judges were no different from a jury.

'They probably wouldn't want to hear that, but you would be a fool to guess which way they would go,' Menzies said. Or how long they would take to decide Maxam's fate.

Cyril put the matter aside and got on with his work. Finally, in mid-March of 1930, the judges found in McAnulty's favour by a majority verdict of three to two. The injunction against the production of Maxam cheese was dissolved. It appears that the case hinged on a seemingly pedantic question of interpretation.

James Kraft had stated in his original patent that the processed cheese was completely sterile and, on the evidence presented to them, the three High Court judges considered this claim to be false. This was despite general agreement that Kraft's cheese was as close to complete sterility as scientifically possible.

Fred Walker cabled news of the decision to the company founder. James Kraft was not a man to leave stones unturned and within a few months Cyril was preparing to depart for London. There, leave would be sought to review the High Court's decision in the Commonwealth's ultimate court of appeal, the Privy Council.

Cyril, Kit and Jean made the voyage to Southampton while my father and his brother were packed off to continue their schooling in Shepparton. Cyril took with him a large chest of documents relating to the appeal, but after arrival in England they set off immediately for a tour of the Continent. The travel itinerary was probably less romantic than my grandmother would have wished, but for Cyril the chance to visit some of the biggest cheese-producing operations in Europe was an opportunity not to be missed.

A large framed print depicting wheels of cheese stacked in towers at the Alkmaar cheese markets in Holland hung in my grandparents' hallway for many years after the trip. Cyril wrote to Reg excitedly describing his visit to the Kraft factory in Rotterdam. There were other cheese-oriented side trips to Switzerland and Germany.

On returning to England, Cyril ventured north to inspect what remained of Gretna Green. He wrote to Reg that the buildings were almost all demolished and the place was desolate and useless – but still there were some memories that could not be erased, that were etched into the very air itself: 'We could still smell the acid fume when wandering among the ruins.'

In fact, Cyril saw the empty ruin of Gretna Green reflected in an entire country:

> The unemployed are increasing, and trade is diminishing. One sees little evidence of it in London but in the manufacturing and country districts … conditions are pitiful.

A letter from Fred Walker confirmed conditions back home were not much better, although sales were being maintained. Cyril knew, however, that chances that this would continue might depend upon his discoveries while away.

While the firm's lawyers played out the lengthy process of petitioning the Privy Council, Kit and Jean took refuge in Annan while Cyril had a few oppportunities to indulge his passion for sport. An inter-university athletics carnival was attended with a 'likeable and level headed Yank' but, more importantly, Australia's national cricket team had just commenced an Ashes Test series against England. Cyril wrote to Reg that Donald Bradman was the talk of the town after amassing a colossal triple century at Headingley, Leeds. Englishmen, he said, had no defence to the Don's precision drilled weaponry:

> They are all scratching their heads to find a way out of trouble. After the second test all the armchair experts

demanded a drastic series of changes, but they practically all agreed that their present team is the best they can muster and now they don't quite know what to do about it.

In London, after what Cyril considered 'much palaver', the petition to seek leave to the Privy Council was finally lodged. As with the cricket, he considered the English legal team to be a poor imitation of their Australian counterparts and no match for Menzies.

> Our appeal as drafted by Menzies did not suit them, but had to be drawn up afresh – although they could not find any fresh points of law on which to base it other than those which Menzies had made.

After discovering blunders in his statements of evidence, Cyril's expectations dwindled. 'We are hoping for the best, but it is not reassuring.' He also observed that the Kraft company in England was so busy looking after its own commercial matters it was unable to spend much time on the appeal.

With the legal business dragging on and an imminent rendezvous with Fred Walker in Chicago, Cyril couldn't wait around. It came as little surprise, however, when he finally received news by cable that the appeal had been dismissed.

Despite the patent having survived a legal challenge in America, British law held it to a more exacting standard. Examination by no fewer than eleven judges from Brisbane to London and a case that lasted nearly four years eventually came down to a matter of a few thousandths of a per cent. No matter which way you cut it, Kraft's cheese was not *completely* sterile, and anecdotal evidence of a block surviving perfectly intact for a decade was insufficient proof that it would 'permanently keep' as stated in the patent. And so Maxam would be allowed to continue to produce their cheese, despite the fact that the manufacturing process itself was obtained through a deceptive act by a former Kraft Walker employee.

Shortly after midnight on 16 August 1930, Fred Walker's voyage across the Pacific came to a sudden, unplanned halt. He and his family were awoken by a disconcerting thud as the broken propeller shaft of the SS *Tahiti* speared through the vessel's hull. She immediately began taking water. The captain rushed to the engine room and was disturbed to see one of his crew already immersed up to his waist, pumping furiously. He returned to the bridge and sent out a mayday. Their only hope was an American mail steamer, the *Ventura*, but it was 460 nautical miles distant, near Rarotonga in the Cook Islands.

Fred went to inspect the engine room himself and found the engineers now up to their necks in water. Almost sixty hours after her hull was punctured, the SS *Tahiti* began to list and preparations were made for her 261 passengers to abandon ship. Limited space aboard the lifeboats prohibited the taking of luggage so Fred filled his pockets with business papers and tied others around his arms and under his coatsleeves.

The ship they abandoned had once transported the brave and ill-fated from the shores of Gallipoli to Marseilles and the horrors beyond. Only three years earlier it had also been involved in the deadliest marine accident ever to take place in Sydney Harbour.

On 3 November 1927, the Union Steamship Company vessel had just departed Circular Quay for New Zealand and America when it collided with a fully-laden passenger ferry, the *Greycliffe*, cutting the smaller vessel in two. Forty of the 120 passengers on board were killed, including six schoolchildren, the science master of Sydney Boys' High School and Australia's first female pilot, Millicent Bryant. The cause of the accident remained contentious, particularly given that it had occurred in calm waters on a clear day with high visibility. Two naval courts of inquiry and a coronial inquest were inconclusive, but witnesses asserted that the larger ship had been travelling too fast and the *Greycliffe* had suddenly, inexplicably, swung across her bow.

Now the SS *Tahiti* would meet her own fate below the seas. Her lifeboats drifted for much of the day before black smoke was spotted low on the horizon. The *Ventura* finally drew alongside to retrieve the relieved survivors. Fred later noted that it had not been a comfortable experience climbing a rope up the side of the ship with his arms enclosed in stiff cylinders of paper.

News of the miraculous mid-Pacific rescue sped stateside ahead of the *Ventura*. When she eventually neared the San Francisco coastline, the sky filled with aeroplanes providing a hero's welcome and dropping garlands of flowers into the water. Once in port, Fred was overwhelmed by the attention he and the other *Tahiti* passengers received. He already considered the shipwreck a thing of the past, but the American media were besotted with the dramatic tale of survival.

Fred was invited to speak live on radio at a banquet and, despite protestations of a hectic schedule, found himself being whisked under motorcycle escort through San Francisco in the largest car he had ever seen. When he arrived at the studio, he turned to his host from the broadcasting company and asked what had prompted such an ostentatious display.

'You said you were busy,' the host replied. It would never, Fred thought, have happened in Australia.

After he delivered his speech, Fred was informed that five million people had listened in. Later he told a more modest number of readers of *CheeseKraft* that he was very glad that he had not known that beforehand.

The Doc

While my grandfather travelled to Chicago, Kit went to stay with family and friends in Annan. Jean attended the local school and my aunt later described the experience as one of the most wonderful times of her life. In the absence of any surviving postcards or letters, it's not clear how the boys back in Australia fared. Years later my father would remark simply that 'the old man was away a lot', predominantly in America.

In August 1930, while Fred Walker was being rescued in the middle of the Pacific, Cyril's ship steamed into the Canadian port of Montreal, taking a route only possible in summer due to the ice jams that turned the navigation channel solid in winter. The whirlwind trip across Canada and the United States was no holiday – it was to be an exhaustive fact-finding mission into the secrets of the rapidly developing American food industry.

From Toronto, Cyril went on to Chicago and then Indiana, across to Philadelphia, New York and out through the Midwest. Was it all work? My cousin remembers seeing a photo from that trip, now lost, of Cyril standing beside the Grand Canyon in Arizona. But looking at the masses of technical reports that survive from his trip, it must have been but the briefest sightseeing interlude.

Nor was it all about cheese. Cyril's fact-finding mission had him poking his nose into whatever type of food manufacturing plant he could find. He visited everything from warehouses in Wisconsin to canneries in California, looking behind lab doors, perusing processes and prowling production lines. His reports describe salad dressings, relishes, fruits, jam, confectionery, and methods of preparing food including blending, rinding, slicing and dicing. Even the packaging and labelling did not escape his scrutiny.

Of course, nothing my grandfather saw remotely resembled his beloved black breakfast spread. There's no record of whether he carried a jar or two with him or cajoled his hosts into giving it a try. If he did, it certainly failed to tempt the American palate, as it does to this day.

It was late 1930 when Kit and Jean finally met up with Cyril in Chicago. My grandfather took a rare day off to celebrate their arrival, but even that meant sailing Lake Michigan on a yacht – with James Kraft at the tiller and, inevitably, business at the helm.

Cyril wrote that their discussions revolved mainly around the rapidly changing economic landscape. The irrepressible American entrepreneur was bullish – his phenomenally popular cheese had laid the foundations for further expansion and no Depression or failed court case was going to stop that. Others had copied his cheese before, but his belief in the power of marketing on which he had built an empire had not diminished.

Even as Cyril and James talked, deals were being finalised by Kraft to sell butter and cheese in Cuba. Australia, with its access to Asia, was seen as an important staging post in the company's plans for global expansion. When the new Kraft Walker factory situated on the banks of the Yarra River in South Melbourne opened, a large photograph of the building graced the front page of the US *CheeseKraft* newsletter in February 1929. Inside was an article that spelled out the company manifesto. Kraft's growth, it declared, required bold thinking and new approaches:

> We are no longer the progressive, aggressive underdog struggling for a place in the sun. Henceforth we shall be looked upon as a great heartless soulless corporation, seeking to accomplish our ends by monopoly rather than quality of product. If we are to be great as well as large, we shall have to develop the fullest measure of cooperation for efficiency. And efficiency we must have, even at the expense of camaraderie and good fellowship.

James Kraft was correct in asserting that the bigger they grew the less their success would be perceived as the result of a focus on quality and innovation. They now ranked among the largest food companies in the world, but there is no doubt that men of small beginnings like Fred and Cyril would have still considered themselves underdogs, accurately or not. All the evidence pointed to them being men who greatly valued friendship and company morale. It seems unlikely that this new ideology would have met with their favour, but the challenges of the Depression were rapidly changing the outlook of industry and governments alike.

Australia's food industry had become increasingly internationalised but, as inflation rose and employment fell, there was an almost hysterical push to buy homegrown goods exclusively. Former prime minister Stanley Bruce had been quoted as saying that to do otherwise would be 'un-Australian', a term he had once earlier used to describe striking seamen.

After what turned out to be an epic voyage of discovery, Cyril, Kit and Jean sailed into Australian shores in late October 1930. They arrived in Sydney to the exciting sight of the new Harbour Bridge, the opposing steel spans of its great cantilevered arch having met only a few months earlier.

When my father and Ian were collected from Shepparton, they each received a few presents, among them an Indian headdress and a pair of tiny wooden clogs. Curiously, the clogs weren't purchased during Cyril's cheese explorations in Holland but rather from a shop in Annan.

The laboratory to which my grandfather returned was among the most sophisticated and well resourced in the country. Armed with his American research and the tools of innovation, Cyril could explore new horizons. He also knew that his past research, particularly his work on the invention of Vegemite, had value beyond the grocer's till. So he initiated a correspondence with the faculty of science at the University of Melbourne in which he sought formal recognition of his endeavours.

A letter to the dean presented Cyril's impressive qualifications: a Bachelor of Science, the Masters degree conferred in absentia while he was at Gretna Green, and a lifetime of laboratory work at Kraft Walker that had been completed in a decade. There was just one problem. All the work my grandfather had undertaken was confidential, commercially precious and prohibited from publication. Cyril knew that to be considered for a doctorate, his work was required to be submitted for public examination.

My grandfather's application for an exemption was refused, yet the correspondence continued. A letter in my possession provides a clue as to how the situation was finally resolved. Ernst Hartung, a university professor and president of the Chemical Institute, explained to Cyril that there was no way of preventing a copy of any submitted work being lodged with the university library. But that in itself did not mean it would necessarily be discovered. It seemed that work lodged in that way was well buried.

> Of course it is accessible to anyone who wishes to see it, and you will know better than I whether you run any danger in this respect from individuals in this city who may happen to know something of University practice.

This was enough for Cyril. He was halfway across the Pacific with Kit and Ian on yet another voyage of discovery when a receipt for ten guineas – the application fee for lodgment of his doctoral thesis – was received by the factory manager at Kraft Walker. The evidence of my grandfather's success is inscribed on his passport where, at some point during his travels, 'Mr' was crossed out in favour of 'Dr'. Cyril's doctorate was the first such higher degree awarded by an Australian university for studies in food science. My father Bill shared the news with all his school friends, who naturally assumed Cyril would attend the next outbreak of measles.

Cyril was proud of his achievement but saddened by the fact that his own schoolmaster father wasn't alive to see it. The framed certificate hung on the wall of our family study with the fossilised fish and the watercolour planes. When my frail father was moving out of his home I rescued it from the waste skip – I knew it was significant but at the time did not know exactly why. The certificate represents a pinnacle achievement of the life of a man who was born to humble circumstance. And it is almost certainly the world's only university degree ever awarded for studies in Vegemite.

It was only a brief six months before Cyril revisited America. As in the previous year, he totted up an impressive list of scientific and industrial investigations. Kit and Ian went sightseeing while Cyril made examinations into thermometers and the practical applications of shatterproof glass. Notes were taken on stainless steel and numerous other more obscure processes.

In my grandfather's reports a random product that had caught his eye – Swanky Swig Cream Cheese – was sandwiched between a visit to an engineer's shop and laboratory tests on rancidity. The 'swanky swig' referred to a type of jar that had begun to appear in the early 1930s that could double as a drinking glass. It was decorated with etched motifs and as years went by these became more elaborate. From this was eventually born that unique item embedded in Australian national consciousness, the 'Vegemite glass' – a ubiquitous drinking vessel that for decades could be found up the back of every Australian family's kitchen cupboard.

Chicago made Kit nervous, and more so on this visit. Newspapers ran thick with the crimes of gangsters, some of whom had already achieved international infamy. Not long before they arrived the psychopathic Baby Face Nelson had quietly slipped out of the city after a murderous spree. Other notorious criminals like Bugs Moran and Al Capone seemed to have even the police quaking in fear. Open machine-gun battles on city streets seemed a far cry from the car-napping exploits of thugs like Squizzy Taylor back in Melbourne. Yet it didn't seem to worry Cyril and a young Ian. Whatever they told my father and Jean when they returned, however, had an impact. Years later those two would talk about it as though they had been there themselves, right in the midst of the bullets, heists and bootleggers. In reality I think it was probably a montage of memories from films, newsreels and radio dramas.

The three Callisters travelled across to New York and checked into the newly opened New Yorker, a modern art deco hotel with an impressive forty-three floors. Above it towered the Chrysler Building which for a fleeting moment, before the Empire State Building shot past into the clouds, had been the world's tallest skyscraper.

Not to be outdone, the New Yorker was the city's largest hotel, with 2500 rooms, ten private dining salons and five restaurants. There were ninety-two telephone operators, 150 laundry staff and a barbershop boasting forty-two chairs. It was all supported by America's largest private power plant and the hotel's guests were reputed to include actors, celebrities, athletes, politicians, mobsters, the shady and the luminous.

At night as Kit and Ian listened to one of four stations on their in-room radio, Cyril would write reports, numbering each before filing them in his briefcase to be typed up on their return. By the time they did, it was nearly summer. They had been away for eight months, but it was enough time for Ian to acquire a stateside twang of great amusement to his siblings and cousins. My father was envious of Ian but consoled himself by telling anybody within earshot that he would be the next to travel and that his adventures would surely eclipse those of his brother.

Cyril was glad to be home and even gladder to be back at work. As he walked the factory corridors and talked to the familiar faces he discovered he had a new nickname. He was now fondly referred to as 'The Doc'.

The situation outside the factory gates had only grown worse in his absence. A steady stream of jobseekers were daily turned away and the nation's unemployment numbers continued to rise unabated, approaching thirty per cent.

Those who already had jobs at Kraft Walker were comforted by the company's surprising prosperity. Yet with household budgets shrinking and infant malnutrition on the rise, there was increasing pressure to develop foodstuffs low in cost but high in nutritional value. Not since the last war had Australia seen such distressing levels of preventable childhood illnesses. Milk supplies were challenged by the inadequacies of refrigeration, leading to contamination and spoiling. It seems reasonable to imagine that somewhere deep down Cyril was anxious to exorcise thoughts of his mother and the tainted cup and the typhoid-riddled urn. He could also see that the field of microbiology was taking on a new importance. His own meticulous examination of the cheese manufacturing process while in America had included exploration of the nutritional aspects of casein and whey. The latter appeared to be especially worthy of evaluation as a potential powdered milk substitute. Along with calcium and phosphorous, whey contained molecules known as amino acids, reputed to possess critical life-sustaining properties.

Cyril also knew that the potential health benefits of Vegemite to date had only been superficially explored. Kraft Walker's sales booklet promoted Vegemite as a 'protective food' but it stopped short of claiming any specific health benefit. The black stuff's best attribute, readers were informed, was its adhesive qualities:

> Children become intensely fond of Vegemite and as they cannot remove it once it is spread, it may be employed usefully in introducing them to new food … they take the new food without demur.

In case that wasn't sufficient to persuade the purchaser, inspired by the words of Stanley Bruce, Kraft Walker made a final plea to the consumer's sense of patriotic duty: 'Vegemite is Australian down to the last detail … Australia doesn't need to import its foodstuffs'.

The suburb of Kew in eastern Melbourne was leafy, middle class and convenient. Robert Menzies had made his home there and so had many of Cyril's business peers. The move from Brighton, however, wasn't without tears. Kit and the children said farewell to their friends and in an instant the beach, the yabbies and their childhood wanderings were over. But Cyril the pragmatist didn't look back. The four-bedroom, two-storey brick house in Kew they moved into had just been completed and came with an adjoining block of land. Cyril hung the picture of the Alkmaar cheese markets in the entry hall beside the door to his study.

Shortly after the move, Cyril returned home from a business trip to find my father and Jean running high fevers. Kit had observed the steady decline and had been frantically trying to contact her husband. They rushed both children to a nearby doctor's surgery, only to return later that night without them.

Polio, or infantile paralysis, was a scourge that had intermittently affected humans for millennia. It was thought that almost all children contracted the polio virus as soon as they were weaned from breast milk, but serious symptoms were rare. With the exception of isolated events it had lain dormant in Australia until the 1920s, but repeated epidemics across the world confirmed fears that the virus had mutated into a vastly more dangerous form.

The doctor examined the Callister children and sent them straight to the Queen's Memorial Hospital, an institution given over almost exclusively to the treatment of infectious diseases. The initial prognosis was heartbreaking. Jean was gravely ill and would fight for her life. Bill was faring better but would need to be kept under close observation. Only Ian had been spared polio's ravages, but he would need to be kept home from school as a precaution and his condition closely monitored.

Cyril sought clinical advice from the best pediatricians in the country but medical research had yet to find a weapon to combat the disease. Polio had been declared a notifiable disease in 1922 but few advances had been made in its prevention or treatment. It was easily spread through contact with polio sufferers or the ingestion of contaminated food or water. Remarkably, however, only one to two per cent of those who were infected actually displayed any symptoms of the disease – but for those who did it could be debilitating.

Polio was an aggressive virus that attacked the lymphoid tissues of the gastrointestinal tract and, in the worst cases, could spread through the bloodstream to the entire central nervous system. The real cruelty of the disease lay in the fact that, for largely unknown reasons, its victims were predominantly young children, some of whom would remain paralysed for life. By the early 1930s, the sight of schoolchildren hobbling about in leg braces or struggling to control limbs deformed by muscle wasting was becoming all too familiar. As it happeneed, the new President of the United States, Franklin D. Roosevelt, had himself contracted the disease at the age of thirty-nine, which was unusual.

Bill came home first, tired and stiff, but, with the exception of a small lump behind his left leg, well. He had survived. Jean remained in hospital for a longer period until the necessary preparations could be made for her care at home. It was there that her medically sanctioned torture began.

Jean's childhood bed was now, on doctor's orders, a hard pine plank. She had suffered paralysis in her right arm and leg. The main object of the wooden bed, however, was treatment of her spinal deformity.

She was fitted with a plaster cast from shoulder to pelvis. In time, her frail body grew and rubbed against the constrict-ing plaster, causing blisters that burnt and stung. After each outgrown cast was discarded and a new one fitted, the blisters would return. The theory was that the resulting immobilisation would help prevent the muscles from tightening and bones from becoming deformed, though the reality was that without exercise muscles simply atrophied and limbs became weak. Plaster casts would, however, remain a common treatment until several years later when a Townsville nurse by the name of Elizabeth Kenny developed a regime comprising the application of heat packs and physical activity. She was ridiculed by government and the medical profession of the day but her results spoke for themselves. It was too late to help Jean but in time the casts and splints would be discarded and Kenny's methods would become the standard treatment for polio paralysis cases across the world.

Visiting teachers from the nearby Methodist college addressed Jean's rapidly failing education and a Mrs Toogood was hired as a tutor. Cyril's spinster sister Minnie, who bore a striking resemblance to the eponymous cartoon mouse, also began a vigil of care for Jean that would last nearly a lifetime.

Minnie, a no-nonsense woman of enormous patience, was also personal secretary to the general manager of the ANZ bank. To help Jean pass the time she gave her a stamp album and to fill it she steamed the stamps from bank correspondence and envelopes brought home from Kraft Walker. Nine months later, when a second album was nearly full, Jean's final plaster cast was removed.

Many years later, Jean's husband, my uncle, penned a memoir that revealed great sadness. I knew from my cousin that Auntie Jean had always been reluctant to appear in photographs. As a child she had spent two irreplaceable years away from school and wore a surgical corset for the rest of her life. Now I learned that she had also suffered post polio syndrome, which may display symptoms similar to chronic fatigue syndrome – fatigue, pain and general muscle weakness – decades after the original infection. I was also told that in her final years Jean suffered terrible depression.

Modern Science

*A*bout this time a woman called Ruth Dunn entered the Callisters' lives. The auburn-haired housekeeper had an uncompromising air and was to remain with the family for many years, only moving on well after both my grandparents had died. In the early days her presence allowed Kit some respite from the burdens of Cyril's regular absences and Jean's care. As Kraft Walker continued to expand, nothing seemed to be more important than my grandfather's research schedule and he spent the Christmas of 1933 thousands of kilometres from his family in California.

In Australia, as elsewhere, cheese was the fuel driving the company forward. The global Depression deepened and production of locally sourced staple foods became an economic imperative. A reliable supply of good quality cheddar became Kraft Walker's first priority. To this end a deal was struck to lease and expand facilities at the Warrnambool Cheese and Butter Co-operative in south-western Victoria. Fire had destroyed the regional factory premises a few years earlier but the new plant at Allansford would soon grow to become one of the biggest bulk cheese facilities in the world. The Kraft Walker Milk and Cheese Factory at Drouin, in West Gippsland, east of Melbourne, was also operating at maximum capacity.

One of Cyril's early recruits, Audrey Osborne, returned to the company in the mid-1930s after separating from her husband and quitting a poorly paid job as chief dietician at one of Melbourne's leading hospitals. Despite the fact that she was a single woman with two children, her job as a microbiologist at Drouin involved working seven days a week. The twins were placed in boarding school, and Audrey would drive the two hours back to Melbourne on Saturday afternoon to see them before returning to Drouin the following morning.

Fred Walker's demands on Cyril also grew. His work overseas had been of enormous value to the company and Cyril offered a pragmatic yet circumspect approach that could bring maturity to all aspects of the business, from engineering to sales. He was sought out for speaking engagements and undertook a constant round of factory visits. All this on top of supervising a raft of research taking place in the company laboratories. The penalty for having become such a critical resource to Kraft Walker's future prospects was a workload that ate away at family life.

Jean still had a noticeable stoop and was yet to return to school. The boys enjoyed attending Scotch College in the inner-eastern suburb of Hawthorn and caught the tram with other children who lived in the same street, some of whom would remain friends for life. Ian was the most outgoing of them all. He excelled at sport, played the piano well and the trumpet, to the annoyance of neighbours, not so well. He was mechanically minded and, perhaps inspired by his adventures in New York, was always building extravagant metal structures out of Meccano.

Both at home and school, my father Bill appeared to live in his brother's shadow. He was left-handed and referred to himself as a mollydooker even though he had been forced to write with his right hand. The children were, however, close, and likely drawn even closer because of Cyril's sacrifice to work and Kit's frequent bouts of illness.

Despite Cyril's professional commitments, the family somehow still managed to take the occasional holiday together. In the study of my parents' home the bottom drawer of my father's antique desk housed a jumble of old black-and-white photographs. Among the dog-eared memories were images with the words 'Buxton', 'Lorne' or 'Cowes' scrawled in pencil on the back.

Cyril loved to drive and my father vividly recalled travelling to the seaside haven of Lorne along the newly opened Great Ocean Road, a tremendous swoop of spine-tingling clifftop tar that leads west below the Otways to Apollo Bay and beyond. It had taken more than a decade for three thousand returned World War I servicemen to hew the spectacular road from the rock with explosives, picks, spades and axes. My father's face assumed a look of awe as he used to recount the backseat rollercoaster ride with Cyril at the wheel.

Interestingly, the new route terminated at Allansford and I

can imagine Cyril deriving as much pleasure from driving to the new Kraft Walker cheese production plant as he did from family vacations.

Fred Walker had suffered from high blood pressure for a number of years, but the sudden death of the energetic businessman in July 1935 at the age of fifty-one shocked all who knew him. Workers at Kraft Walker were upset and an air of uncertainty and disbelief pervaded the company for more than a year afterwards.

On 24 July 1935 the *Argus* reported 'a large attendance' at Walker's funeral which was held at his home in Harcourt Street, Auburn. When the procession moved on to the cemetery, the route was lined with company employees, some overcome with grief. The pallbearers were Fred's close friends and associates, one of whom was my grandfather. Fred was in good company at Boroondara General Cemetery in Kew – among the other residents were early Australian entrepreneurs including a mausoleum housing the founder of the *Age* newspaper, David Syme, and the father of Australian Rules football, Henry Harrison. Four cars were used to ferry the flowers.

Some years later Cyril wrote a tribute to his patron and colleague in *CheeseKraft*. It listed Walker's achievements though it lacked the intimacy one might have expected between two men who had worked so closely together. The American operation now took the opportunity to complete the merger that it had commenced seven years earlier and secured a controlling interest in its Australian cousin. Cyril was appointed a director and given formal charge of all technical and production matters.

There is no doubt that Fred Walker's death placed even greater responsibility on my grandfather's shoulders, but these seemed to have been better days for the family. Jean returned to school – albeit three inches shorter and two grades lower. Ian revelled in sport, music and girls. Indeed, my father often recalled how popular his older brother was and his confidence, intelligence and practical nature won a special place in Cyril's heart.

On the national stage, the conservative PM Joe Lyons also remained popular but Robert Menzies, now the federal member for Kooyong, was being touted as a potential successor. Menzies and my grandfather maintained a close friendship. They both attended the local Presbyterian church, and Cyril occupied a seat on its board of management. Cyril ran fundraisers at which he would present lectures and exhibit photographic slides of his travels. He told his family that many of the board members frustrated him because they weren't businessmen and were loath to make decisions.

Over the next year Cyril continued to look among the best and brightest for successors, searching out young scientists who could take up the challenges of research in the laboratories from which he was increasingly absent. One of those he identified, Derek Shew, remembered being courted and then persuaded to join Kraft Walker. In a letter to my father he described how he had initially resisted Cyril's advances:

> I had just obtained my degree in Agricultural Science and was working on a research grant in the dairy research lab at the veterinary research institute. One day your father, whom I had never met, phoned and asked if I could call and see him. I was very busy at the time and had the temerity to tell him I could not. So he came to see

me and that is how he offered me the job. We were all encouraged to write research reports and present them at meetings of the research committee. He took a great interest in this work but his comments were direct and incisive. We were kept up to the mark! At the same time he was a shrewd businessman.

Cyril was one of Derek Shew's dairy industry heroes. When he was recruited he was undertaking postgraduate work in bacteriology and Cyril sent him to Allansford to work for another of his protégés, Theo Easton.

It turned out to be a masterstroke. At the time, cheese production in Australia and New Zealand was under threat from bacteriophage, a viral disease of cheese starters. An infected vat could wipe out a day's production in a matter of hours and if left unchecked, the biological nightmare had the potential to rapidly spread through an entire factory and cripple an industry.

Shew led the research work at Allansford in close liaison with industry professionals from all over Australasia. The Palmerston North Dairy Institute in New Zealand was one of the largest in the world and together with Kraft advances were made in controlling and quarantining the virus.

The company's rapidly escalating reputation as a leader in food science saw others frequently seek their assistance and advice. Very few competitors could boast the research and testing capacity that Cyril and Fred had developed, and Cyril also worked at keeping communication channels open with the CSIR scientists.

On one occasion, the factory manager Frank Daniel entered Cyril's laboratory carrying a half-eaten jar of apple jelly. A friend of his, the general manager of the Australian Jam Company (AJC), had given it to him. The problem was, Frank told the chemists, that an elderly customer had complained that the jelly made her teeth go black. The challenge held no fear for lab staff accustomed to the horrors of sampling rancid cheese or failed batches of yeast extract.

A cursory sniff and taste revealed a metallic taint and the case was quickly declared solved. Small amounts of iron had somehow leached from the production equipment and into the jam. But that was not enough to turn teeth black. It was only when the lady had eaten her bread and jelly while sipping on a cup of tea that the metal had reacted with the tea's tannin to produce an inky residue. Daniel told his friend that the AJC would need to consider replacing their equipment with stainless steel to avoid future outbreaks of 'blacktooth'.

Encouraged by Cyril and his resourceful staff, Daniel began to examine other potential uses for his factory's products. It was known that lactose could be used to make a product similar to Bakelite, a precursor to plastic, and casein could be used in paint. Now Daniel recruited staff to experiment with similar possibilities using whey powder. So fascinated did he become with the process that a worker discovered him secreted away in the lab one day cooking up his own witches' brew, randomly adding various chemicals to the whey as it heated. Fortunately, the worker was able to discourage Daniel from proceeding any further, narrowly averting disaster.

A colleague once described Frank Daniel as being a man of infinite ideas, some good and some bad. Only Cyril, he said, had the ability to discern which of them were workable and which were not.

It was true that the development of new products was key to the company's future, but so too was promotion of the company's existing product lines. At least Vegemite was free of suggestions that it stained consumers' teeth! And yet, no amount of advertising seemed able to inspire a surge in popularity. Numerous nationwide campaigns extolling the spread's nutritional virtues and its ability to encourage children to eat unwanted vegetables were having little impact. Jars were being given away with cheese and other Kraft products, and even the lure of winning a new Pontiac car had failed to drive sales.

In the words of Kraft's own salesmen, the figures were going nowhere.

At the same time, other companies and products were successfully riding the wave of mechanisation, expansion and the implementation of modern marketing methods. The confectionery company MacRobertson's in Melbourne's Fitzroy employed two and a half thousand people in factory premises spread across a thirty-acre block. The Swallow & Ariell Ltd factory in Port Melbourne produced more than two hundred varieties of biscuits, cakes and puddings, proudly boasting that all were untouched by human hand until they reached the packaging line.

Heinz, another American company, had recently set up shop in inner-city Richmond to produce its famous '57 Varieties' of canned soups, baked beans and sauces. The Swiss firm Nestlé, which had been manufacturing in Australia since 1918, had now started domestic production of its popular 'Fortified Tonic' beverage known as Milo. Sanitarium acquired the rights to a competitor of its own breakfast biscuit, and the product it subsequently marketed as Weet-Bix became a runaway success.

In Sydney, an enterprising tram conductor named Bert

Appleroth made jelly crystals from sugar and gelatine in his bathtub. By eventually forsaking his tram-based distribution system for a plane he named Bertie, Appleroth made Aeroplane Jelly a household name. The jingle that first went to air on Radio 2KY in Sydney in 1930 – sung by an actress mimicking a child's voice – was so catchy that it was played on radio more than one hundred times per day. Eighty years later it would still be in circulation. Assisted by bold publicity stunts, including using a Tiger Moth to distribute his product to rural areas, model aeroplane displays in Sydney's Centennial Park and the airdropping of jelly packets over Bondi Beach, sales for this product soared into the stratosphere.

Competition for household attention was propelling the invention of many products that remain popular to this day. Food manufacturers keen to increase sales and satisfy the diverse appetites of the nation were assisted by CSIR's efforts to overcome the many challenges of mass food production. Despite advances of the previous decade, cold storage and preservation methods were still imperfect and together with the eradication of pests and disease, these remained the top priorities for the scientists.

When my father decided it was time for me to look after any Vegemite-related matters, I asked him first to contact a few of Cyril's colleagues and friends to collect impressions of the man. Many of my grandfather's colleagues' replies began with phrases like 'I can see him now'. Their memories seemed remarkably undimmed by time and all manner of detail spilled forth.

Friends, on the other hand, would mostly reply that while

they had given the matter a lot of thought, they recalled very little that might help 'define' him. It seems that Cyril the man was defined by his work.

That said, one of his early friends, Bob Sinclair, told my father that he had been the recipient of an act of generosity that continued to resonate to this day:

> The one thing that I will always remember your father for, which I will forever be grateful, was that he gave me his bicycle. I do not remember the circumstances, or why, all I know was I was the proud owner of his bicycle. Over the years I have told many people about this bike … an English Humber. I must have travelled thousands of miles … I took it to the Mallee where I worked for a couple of months during the Depression … My eldest son next rode it and he passed it down to my younger son, who eventually gave it to the young brother of a girl he was going with. I will always remember your father for the hours of enjoyment that bike gave me.

Bert Gilbert worked as Cyril's personal assistant and sought me out at a family occasion to tell me how much I looked like my grandfather. 'But,' he added, 'I'll bet you're glad not to have been named Cyril or Percy!' He was right.

Bert was engaging and charming. He spoke highly of Cyril, whom he said was able to command the loyalty of those closest to him and, in most cases, persuade them to perform at their peak. He also had the uncanny ability of sifting the chaff from the grain. That was what made Cyril and the mercurial Frank Daniel such a formidable pair of operators.

There were, it seemed, many sides to Cyril Callister and he was certainly a man with a passion for all manner of scientific subjects. Despite his outwardly conservative nature, he possessed many ideas that were well ahead of his time. An excerpt from the proceedings of the Royal Australian Chemical Institute cites a conversation that Cyril had in the 1930s regarding water. Apparently he had raised the possibility of reversing the flow of the Murray River and introduced the controversial topic of desalination. Even at that time the author commented that these suggestions were possibly not so silly as they sounded.

Boiling Point

At the age of ninety-three, Cyril's longtime colleague Keith Farrer had witnessed many great events of the last century When we sat down to talk at length he soon guided me on a detailed journey across the years he had known my grandfather. In his youth, Farrer was quite the Renaissance man: he had come close to running the four-minute mile and he possessed a distinguished academic record.

A week before his twenty-second birthday, Cyril offered Farrer a job at Kraft Walker at the going rate of £6 per week with two weeks' annual leave. He had recently completed his masters degree in science and accepted. He reported to work at the building on the Yarra River called Riverside, where South-bank now stands. He had studied chemistry intensively for more than four years but by his own admission knew nothing about food analysis. Although all but one of the ten laboratory staff was female, Farrer was happy to acknowledge their superior expertise and seek their advice.

On one of those first mornings he was standing at the sampling table waiting for Cyril to arrive when Frank Daniel, adorned in a white lab coat, turned to him.

'So you're the new chemist, are you? Don't think we can't do what you have come to do, it's just that we haven't got time.'

Kraft employees are a proud lot and it seems Daniel just wanted to make sure that Farrer knew this.

After serving his apprenticeship in the lab and undertaking an extended tour of duty at Allansford, Farrer began reporting almost exclusively to Cyril.

He soon discovered that my grandfather was a man who took all his responsibilities seriously; a perfectionist for whom close enough was never good enough. It was a trait forged in the explosive environs of Gretna Green, where the slightest misjudgment would have led to catastrophe. The failed patent case against Maxam cheese, determined by the most minuscule of margins, had further steeled Cyril's outlook.

A short time after returning from Allansford, Cyril instructed Farrer to meet with the government's chief chemist to perform an analysis on Swiss cheese. The offending batch had reputedly failed to meet the minimum requirement of having a fat content of twenty-five per cent.

They repeated the test and the result was 0.1 per cent shy of the mark at 24.9 per cent fat. Farrer returned to Kraft to report his findings. He told Cyril he was sorry but that he was unable to give him the answer that he wanted.

'I meant it as a joke,' Farrer recalled, 'but Cyril gave me the full blast of his pale blue eyes and said, "Keith, we want the truth." It was clear that one did not joke about that sort of thing.'

Farrer went on to say that while The Doc would laugh at a joke, he wasn't one to tell one. He expected dedication and high standards and led by example.

Yet Cyril wasn't entirely devoid of humour. One afternoon The Doc had gone out and a number of workers had started up a game of cricket in the factory corridors. The game proved so entertaining that it extended beyond the lunch break. A worker who asked when Cyril would return was told that they would be warned by the sound of his car.

'No you won't,' came a voice from the other end of the corridor. 'I caught the tram.' Cyril walked past without uttering another word and they all scurried back to work.

'Of course,' Farrer continued, 'there was also the time I nearly killed your grandfather. I remember it well. It was Black Friday, 1939.'

As children, we Callisters often holidayed at Buxton and Marysville, both towns around one hundred kilometres north-east of Melbourne. Marysville had originated as a staging point along the track to the northern goldfields in the late nineteenth century. As you travelled down from the Black Spur and across the Dividing Range you came to Narbethong, a tiny forest-encircled town that had been totally wiped out in 1939. About seventy people had died that day, which until 2009 was the worst bushfire in Australia's records.

'We had a delivery of ether that morning and it was placed on the bench in the lab,' Farrer continued his story:

In those days there was no air conditioning and the lab wall faced to the north. The temperature outside was well over 100 degrees Fahrenheit [38°C]. It actually spiked at 114 degrees [46°C]. I don't know why the ether had been left unattended. When I walked into the laboratory the big flask was sitting on the bench, trembling violently. There was no one else about at the time. It had stood in the morning sun and the contents were boiling. Somehow I managed to get it into the fuming cupboard and as I was running out of the door, your grandfather was coming in. I pushed him out as the ether exploded. As we untangled ourselves, I suggested we go in and see what was left of the lab. Fortunately it was fairly unscathed, but the fuming cupboard was destroyed.

My brother-in-law James, a chemical engineer, later told me that ether boils at only 34.6 degrees Celsius.

It was not until early 1937 that sales for Vegemite began to show signs of life. Baby health centres had continued to push for better infant diets and were now promoting the product to mothers.

Keen to bolster Vegemite's nutritional credentials, Cyril sent a sample to a colleague in London, Professor Katherine Coward, for examination. After exhaustive tests on rats and pigeons, Coward confirmed the presence of aneurin, now better understood as thiamin or vitamin B1.

These results gave Cyril a clear road forward.

Buoyed, he asked Farrer to determine the level of the vitamin in Vegemite using the new thiocrome test. It revealed that the amount of vitamin B1 in the finished product was only half of that found in the raw material. Farrer discovered that if he removed all unnecessary temperature peaks during the yeast extraction process, the vitamin content could be doubled. The observations produced would, with Cyril's encouragement, lead to Farrer gaining his own doctorate in science a few years later.

The significance of the test results was not lost on Kraft Walker's marketing experts. Fresh advertisements rolled out promoting the virtues of the vitamin-packed superfood. One four-ounce jar of Vegemite, it was confidently asserted, contained more vitamin B than three loaves of bread, one bunch of carrots, one lettuce, six apples, six pears, two pints of milk, two plates of porridge, six bananas, one dozen eggs and a pound of peas, potatoes and steak put together.

An image of a rosy-cheeked baby was accompanied by copy worthy of the popular comic book hero Superman himself:

Everyone needs Vegemite. B1 for nerves of steel, B2 for sturdy growth and PP for clear healthy skin.

PP is more commonly known as niacin or vitamin B3. According to Farrer, Cyril scrutinised all advertising copy before it went to print, ensuring that it conformed to his strict standards of scientific veracity. Nerves of steel, it seemed, met the criteria.

Another advertisement boasted a picture of a woman playing tennis. In one corner was an open jar of Vegemite and the banner read, 'Vegemite for vitality … A good serve'.

Incidentally, tennis was becoming increasingly popular in

Australia and around this time my father remembered Cyril buying the house next door and proudly announcing he intended to knock it down and install a court. The neighbours weren't pleased but the plans went ahead.

Elsewhere, events on the world stage were now a matter for serious concern. The woes of the Depression were fast merging into the threat of a new world war. Japan had invaded China and Korea but in Australia politicians still courted Japanese diplomats and favoured appeasement. In Europe, Germany had begun aggressively annexing neighbouring territory.

Before the tennis court was finished, and after Robert Menzies became prime minister, my grandfather suffered a sudden, near-fatal heart attack. Nobody was more shocked than he was. He was forty-six years old.

Cyril was forced to spend quite some time recovering in hospital. Visitors, including the nation's new leader, came and went. He was eventually discharged and instructed to recuperate at home, but by all accounts his constant, demanding presence threw the household into disarray. My grandfather was not a man accustomed to being a mere observer, though now he had no choice. He put a mirror in the study so he could watch his children play tennis, on a court on which it seems he knew he would never now play.

Eventually he returned to work at Kraft Walker on a reduced schedule, insisting Jean leave her new job at the Kew Library to become his personal chauffeur. Each day she would drop him off at Riverside Avenue about 10 am and return to collect him in the early afternoon.

Perhaps such an imposition may have been seen as simply a matter of obligation in those times, but years later my aunt and her family still considered it unfair. After suffering the debilitating strictures of polio Jean had returned to school, had made new friends in the lower grades and even started to play tennis again. Her greatest achievement to date was her job at the local library, which had given her a sense of engagement, freedom and independence. She would miss this job for the rest of her life.

My father loved listening to the radio as a child and many an afternoon in Brighton he would run over to a friend's house across the road to listen to his favourite serials. Cyril would tease him when he returned and call him 'pot o' fish' after a popular children's radio show of the time. When the family moved to Kew they had their own radio and, like many families, would gather together in the evening to avidly listen to the 'wireless'.

It was around the family radio in September 1939 that my father recalled listening in disbelief to a broadcast address by Cyril's old friend, Robert Menzies, an address that my grandfather had known was inevitable. 'Just like that we were at war,' my father later told me. 'I was still at school and Ian was about to finish.'

Soon thereafter, Keith Farrer met with a man whose responsibility it would be to establish an army catering corps. Professor Cedric Stanton Hicks, son of a factory worker, had grown up in New Zealand but had gone on to study medicine and chemistry at Cambridge University. He then took a job as professor of human physiology at the University of Adelaide with a sense of duty to the greater good. As a member of the government's advisory council on food he visited the desert centre several times to study the physiology of Aboriginal men and women. He had also conducted a study of the effects of the Depression on more than five hundred Australian families. Now Hicks had been commissioned to use his scientific expertise to ensure that Australian troops marched on stomachs filled with something more nutritious than bully beef and biscuits.

The same man would years later detail his trials and tribulations in a book titled *Who Called the Cook a Bastard?* This was an old World War I catch-cry that would be met by the rejoinder, 'Who called the bastard a cook!' It reflected the low respect accorded army food that persevered at the start of the next war. Hicks, like Napoleon before him, knew that good nutrition was essential to maintaining the soldiers' health and sustaining a war effort.

The results of Farrer's Vegemite vitamin tests had reached the professor's desk and Hicks contacted him to arrange a meeting. Hicks was keen to include a product rich in vitamin B in army rations. It would complement blackcurrant concentrate for vitamin C and margarine fortified with vitamins A and D.

With a simple stroke of a pen, Cedric Stanton Hicks sent Vegemite to war. That single act would eventually achieve what no amount of advertising could – a permanent place for Vegemite in the national diet. It created the impetus for mass production and provided, through Australia's enlisted troops, a captive market. In the meantime, ever more stringent food rationing would drive demand at home.

Cyril was responsible for much of the organisation of Kraft Walker's war food effort. This included feeding the prime minister who, on occasion, visited the Callister home for lunch.

At Kraft Walker, the carpenters were busy installing timber

shutters over external windows. Production schedules were adjusted and ration pack products prioritised. Cheese came off the conveyor lines in twelve-ounce army cans rather than the familiar blue cartons. Canned meat and Vegemite production was ramped up to fulfil ration requirements. Hicks's new ration packs would also include wheatgerm, chocolate, tea, sugar, wholemeal biscuits, cigarettes and matches. The combination would prove popular with the troops.

A number of key Kraft Walker personnel had already notified management of their intention to join up but the government had learned the lessons of the previous war and acted swiftly to prevent an exodus of workers from essential industries. The navy and airforce commenced a mad scramble to arm and equip. The RAAF instigated the Empire Air Training Scheme to recruit and train pilots.

The lives of those left at home changed rapidly and dramatically. A day's butter ration was no more than a tablespoon. Smokers often went without and even beer was in short supply. If you were one of those who had acquired a taste for Vegemite it now became scarce or unavailable. In its place appeared a new product called Globex – a putrid yellow muck parading as beef extract that was almost inedible. The standing joke was that it must have been made by the enemy for the sole purpose of demoralising Australians.

Austerity had arrived by government decree. The National Security Act was rushed through parliament and gave the government far-reaching controls. Civil rights took a back seat as a war-panicked executive legislated on the run. The Communist Party was banned and more than a thousand conscientious objectors imprisoned. Only a small group of pacifists considered that war was anything but the only option. In the wider community, there was a growing fear that Australia was isolated and vulnerable.

Cyril had a charcoal-burning gas producer fitted to his car to supplement the meagre fuel ration. He was now well enough to take the tram to work while Jean took on a new job and joined the Voluntary Aid Detachment. Ian achieved high marks in his final school exams but deferred university studies in chemical engineering to work at Kraft Walker.

War had taken the Australian food industry by surprise. Many companies still had little understanding of the nutritional value of the products they manufactured. Kraft Walker was better prepared than many and Cyril was determined that they should continue to lead the way.

He set up a new microbiology lab, taking advantage of the scientific talents of an Englishwoman who had been left stranded in Australia by the war. Joyce Griffiths was a graduate from Reading University with impeccable credentials. She was joined soon after by a University of Melbourne microbiology graduate by the name of Margaret Dick. Farrer once again found himself the student of his female colleagues as Cyril instructed him to turn his attentions to microbiology.

In Europe, Hitler's forces swept all before them and messages decoded by defence analysts forewarned of an imminent invasion of England. There was talk in some circles of a negotiated settlement with the Germans, but Churchill refused and prepared Britain and her allies for a long engagement.

The corridors at the Kraft Walker factory were stacked so high with ration-packaged food that the workers could barely move past them. Cyril had made a reasonable recovery but was still constrained to reduced hours and duties. Ian was outworking the tag of being The Doc's son, but wrestled with his conscience over joining up. In early 1941, when he left Kraft Walker and enlisted, the factory engineers reluctantly bid him farewell.

Cyril had held Ian back as long as he could but knew that, like himself, his eldest son was not one to watch life happen from the stands. My grandfather would later recall the enormous release that Ian experienced in joining up:

> During that bad year he was greatly exercised in mind and troubled in spirit as he was eighteen in March and felt already that he should be in the services. After his decision was taken he seemed to know an exaltation of spirit and a serenity of soul, which never afterwards left him.

Up in the Air

It seems in keeping with Ian Callister's vivacious nature that he should have chosen to take to the air. In fact, it fits almost too neatly with those cinematic portraits of war pilots as high-spirited, strong-jawed mavericks whose valour was always accompanied by a guess-who'll-get-the-girl swagger. The stereotype was supported by the fact that some of Hollywood's leading men, such as Jimmy Stewart and Clark Gable, personally flew World War II combat missions.

Ian's enlistment is remembered in a letter from the mayor and citizens of the City of Kew, addressed to Aircraftsman Callister and recording 'with appreciation and pride' his decision to take up active service in defence of Australia and Empire. It was accompanied by the gift of a wallet.

Ian's excitement was tempered only by the bus running out of petrol en route to the base at Somers, on the edge of Westernport Bay. Here, a short stroll from the beach, he took up residence at the No. 1 Initial Training School RAAF for Air Crew and was issued with his kit, which included two floppy fatigue uniforms known as 'giggle suits'.

He told Cyril that he had no spare time: his intake was rushed through basic training in one month. He was inoculated against typhoid and compelled to swot for tests in Morse, administration, maths, electrical science, armoury, gas and drill. He shared a hut with twenty-five other enlistees, slept on an iron stretcher and, like most young men away from home, lamented the fact that he had to do his own washing and ironing. He cheerfully informed his father that he had suffered no ill-effects from the vaccination, was in 'the pink' and slept 'like a top'.

Ian's stay at Somers ended up lasting two months. He was then loaded into a train with the other novices and transported to the central New South Wales town of Temora. He slept as best he could, curled up in the luggage rack, braced against the cold. When they arrived it was a clear night, marred only by the dust of the convoy as they were ferried to No. 10 Elementary Flying School, on the outskirts of town.

Ian wrote home that the food was better at Temora than Somers and the washrooms not as crowded. There were two courses of about sixty pilots, junior and advanced. Only two days after he arrived he had his first aerial 'flip', describing it as 'a wonderful sensation'. A number of the other trainees couldn't hang on to their breakfast and Ian admitted to going close, fumbling under his flying suit for his beret as the plane rolled in the sky.

In response to a telegram from Cyril, he painted a vivid picture of his new life:

> We now get up at 3:45 a.m. every morning. I was flying at 5.15 a.m. this morning and was up before the sun had risen. The sunrise was beautiful ... like a huge red ball creeping over a range of hills to the east of the camp ... the whole skyline was a mass of colours ranging from gold to dark red.

As exhilarating as it was for Ian, there was no doubt about the anxiety my grandparents must have felt for their newly airborne son. Ian was also conscious of this as, at the end of his letter, he added that he hoped he hadn't caused any undue worry. If they had known he was about to undertake his first solo flight with a total of only seven hours of instruction under his belt, any worry they felt would have been entirely justified. As it was, the twenty-minute journey at the controls of a Tiger Moth went without a hitch.

A few days later my father quietly celebrated his eighteenth birthday with the family at home. He had left school and had been working for most of the year at Kraft Walker, though he had struggled to find his niche and moved on from one department to the next. He was also now free to join up or, sooner or later, be called up.

Cyril had seen how the first casualties of war had shaken the close-knit community of workers at Kraft Walker. The grim reality of a continually escalating conflict was impossible to ignore and tensions were high. People the family knew and loved were deployed all over the world – Cyril's youngest brother

Ralph even found himself under siege in the North African port city of Tobruk.

Ian successfully completed his elementary flight training and returned home to Melbourne before being posted to an embarkation depot at Bradfield Park on Sydney's north shore. While awaiting his orders there he took weekend leave and went to stay with his Uncle Reg in the southern suburb of Bexley, hoping to go swimming at Cronulla Beach. Ian remarked that he thought Uncle Reg, a man barely fifty, was looking 'old and tired'.

Reg's daughter, Margaret, now in her eighties and still living in the same suburb, clearly remembered the visit. Ian's cousin Ralph had stayed around the same period before he left for England to become a navigator on Lancaster bombers and Ian had asked Cyril to find out where he was located overseas so they could catch up.

Ralph was eventually posted to a bomber squadron that undertook a number of raids on German industrial cities. Tragically, his plane was shot down on a bombing run over Hamburg, a few months shy of war's end, and he was never seen again. It was to have been his fourth-last mission.

Margaret remembers Cyril and his brothers as 'wonderful gentlemen' and Ian and Ralph as 'the same lovely boys'. Even after nearly seventy years the memory of them clearly wrung her heart.

Ian departed Sydney Harbour bound for Canada in late 1941 under naval escort on the SS *Monterey*. Remarkably, it was a sister ship to the *Mariposa*, upon which Cyril had often crossed the Pacific in the service of Kraft Walker. War had now made this journey far more perilous. Ian sent a brochure from the converted passenger liner for his father's interest, but the censor's razor blade excised both the ship's name and half a page of his accompanying letter. The same wary knife removed mention of the SS *Monterey*'s first port of call but, as Ian remarked to his father, it should have been fairly obvious where they were, given the Maori welcome they received. The censor appeared less interested in Ian's exhaustive description of the various cheeses he encountered during their layover. Gorgonzola, Roquefort, domestic Swiss and more were sampled but none met with approval:

> Some of them look nothing like cheese and have an awful smell … I hope you'll stick to the good plain Cheddar. I can't imagine Kraft's name on some of the things called cheese here.

The SS *Monterey* left New Zealand and its war-bound passengers opened the parcels they had received from the comforts fund. Ian's included a sheepskin jacket, socks, jerseys and gloves, but the ship's recreational schedule was sufficient to keep warm blood running through his veins. There were two exercise classes a day, backed up with a mile run around B deck.

In the last days of November 1941 they sailed into a Honolulu bay crowded with the amassed might of the US Navy's Pacific Fleet, including eight battleships. Numerous aircraft carriers also greeted the gobsmacked young pilots. Within a week all but the carriers would be sunk or destroyed as Japan launched a devastating ambush against a nation not yet at war.

Like everyone else, Cyril was stunned when the radio relayed news of the Pearl Harbor attack. He knew from his own travels that Ian's ship must have been somewhere in close vicinity. To his relief, a telegram arrived soon after the news broke: 'Arrived Canada. Hold mail.'

The SS *Monterey*'s stay in Hawaii had been mercifully short. It reached port in Ontario on 7 December 1941, a date that US President Roosevelt declared would live forever in infamy. The following day Japanese forces attacked Hong Kong, Guam and the Philippines. Events went from bad to catastrophic. Within days the Royal Navy had lost its warships, the *Prince of Wales* and the *Repulse*, off the coast of Malaya. There was now no allied naval presence of any significance in the Asia Pacific region. Within three months Singapore had fallen and Darwin had been bombed. The nightmare had come true. Australia was vulnerable, isolated and in danger. The war over there was *here*, and frighteningly near.

After the Japanese brought the Americans into the war, US Army officials and servicemen arrived in Melbourne en masse. Cyril attended numerous meetings as the Americans came to Kraft with a host of new demands. Some of these were satisfied by a simple change in product and an increase in output. Others, like the dehydration of vegetables, required a whole new technology. There was no time for product development. Problems were solved on the run or not at all.

Into the lab and onto the factory floor came university people and military personnel briefed to oversee the manufacture of American rations. Several worked directly alongside Farrer, who would later refer to the war as the first important external stimulus to food research in Australia.

The Pacific situation was also bringing Australia to the eyes of the world. From Canada, Ian wrote that he had seen many articles and newsreels featuring his hometown:

> Last night we saw Gen MacArthur arriving at Spencer St station and driving to the Menzies Hotel. We get quite a kick whenever we see parts of Melbourne like that.

Many at home were reassured by General Douglas MacArthur's assessment that he doubted Japan's capacity to invade Australia. It was coupled, however, with the sombre observation that an invasion of New Guinea could give the enemy a base from which to launch an attack.

It was about this time that Cyril began to work on an air raid shelter in the backyard of the family home. He sent a picture of the work-in-progress to Ian, who replied that it looked like a 'smart job'. He added, however, that it was a pity that a section of lawn had to be dug up. But by the middle of 1942 the building of backyard air raid shelters was becoming a common sight across the country.

With Japanese midget submarines detected in Sydney Harbour and the port of Newcastle, war was literally on Australia's doorstep. The conflict in New Guinea was also about to commence in earnest and, as troop numbers multiplied, increased supplies of food were required to be dispatched north. Tropical heat and the vagaries of war made it a difficult task to ensure the food arrived intact, in time or at all. Rations were moved from overcrowded wharves and remote beach-heads up through the dense jungle tracks and beyond.

Where possible, supplies were dropped in by aircraft, often

referred to as 'biscuit bombers'. In the isolated and remote villages of the New Guinea highlands, the most wonderful and exotic goods fell from the sky. Sugar and chocolate were well received, but Vegemite may well have proven too much for the local palate. It wasn't long, however, before the Japanese interrupted supply by bombing and strafing the harbour and airfields in Port Moresby.

In the early days of combat, before reinforcements arrived, Australian reservists fought a retreating battle against the Japanese forces. But, like the Australians, the Japanese resources were stretched and their own supplies often amounted to no more than a small ration of rice and whatever they could pilfer from the locals. The further they pushed their enemy back through the jungle, the more critical supply became.

In consultation with Cyril and his food industry colleagues, Cedric Stanton Hicks made changes to the basic ration pack to render it more appropriate to conditions. In Melbourne, Kraft's chemists and microbiologists were working overtime to overcome new problems. Many of the lab staff had been hand-picked by Cyril for their academic gifts, but he could never have envisaged the problems that war would throw at them.

The rare but devastating paralytic illness botulism was a common problem, generally caused by cans being pierced by rough handling or shrapnel. In some cases the damage was deliberate, a crude form of biological warfare as Australian troops tampered with supplies and left them to be consumed by the starving Japanese in their pursuit.

There was also the odd exploding can of Vegemite, but this was not an attempt to bring the yeast extract into the front line. Kraft's microbiologists suspected tainted product or some kind of bacterial reaction. Finding nothing, they passed the problem over to the chemists. Finally it was discovered that the reason lay with the very stuff that gave Vegemite its flavour, a reaction between sugars and amino acids that caused the cans to blow. Keith Farrer discussed the problem with Cyril and was left to solve it. It was a Maillard reaction, he reported, and quite simple to fix.

In 1942, Ian's family received a letter from Kit's cousin Bella in Canada. At the time of writing, she said it was 42 degrees below zero and she wondered how Ian and his colleagues were coping.

From Ian's letters home it seemed that he was coping well, enjoying the unfamiliar pastimes of ice skating and skiing. He thought the Canadians must have had a keen sense of balance because one of the chaps from their course was always flat on his back on the ice. He also enjoyed spending time with other servicemen from all over the Commonwealth and told his parents that they teased each other over their native speech:

> There are chaps here who say 'what' after each sentence just like dad did after he returned from his last visit to America. A lot of the Canadians say 'eh' after each sentence.

A constant stream of letters flew across the Pacific, but only rarely did Ian voice concern about the conflict into which he was about to be thrust:

Things aren't so good, we've certainly been taking all the knocks of this war but I am certain we'll paste hell out of the Huns and the Japs before the war is over.

More often he described a life full of flying, dances and food:

I had my first flip in a Yale. There is a lot more to it than the old Tiger. The things used that weren't in the Tiger are flaps, mixture control, variable pitch, gyro compass and artificial horizon, brakes (applied by pressure on top of the rudder controls), vertical speed indicator, boost control plus many other minor points to be watched. The altimeter, boost and airspeed indicator are graduated in kilometers and the wording is in French.

The technical details were no doubt to satisfy Cyril's scientific bent, but other passages would have been of more interest to his mother:

We have been issued with long winter underpants. I thought I would be an old man before I wore them but I changed into them the last cold spell we had and have been wearing them since.

The food supply chain to Canada, it transpired, was also more reliable than to Australia's north. A fruitcake sent by sister Jean was eaten with sentimental relish – 'every time I have a bite of it, it reminds me of home' – and a big hamper arrived courtesy of the Kraft social club. In return, Ian sent his Uncle Ralph a carton of cigarettes given him by the Anzac Club in New York.

In April 1942, Ian spent four and a half days on leave in the Big Apple. On his first afternoon he visited Radio City and after touring the facilities, cut a record with his friends to be relayed back to Australia. He then moved onto the NBC television studios before heading out to dinner at a place called Longchamps where, he reported, there was a dancefloor in the middle of the room and each chap had a girl to look after him. Ian and his friends savoured every moment, pursuing the hurried itinerary of men for whom most pleasures would soon be denied.

> The next morning we went to the Empire State Building. The visibility was about fifteen miles [twenty-five kilometres]. Boy, it's a most fantastic sight isn't it. You could see the *Normandie* lying helplessly on her side in the Hudson River. She reminded me of a horse that got bogged in the mud in Gardiners creek one time ...

Along with the *Queen Elizabeth* and the *Queen Mary*, the *Normandie* was one of the world's three largest ships. She had captured the Atlantic speed record on her maiden voyage and later successfully avoided the German U-boats on her journey to America. There, while it was being converted into a troop carrier, an absent-minded welder managed to achieve what the enemy could not. A spark from his torch set alight a cargo of spare lifejackets stored in the first-class lounge. The ship's extinguishing system had been disconnected, fire spread rapidly and eventually, after a farcical series of attempts to get the blaze under control, the *Normandie* keeled over on her port side. That very night Ian went to the Stage Door canteen where girls and the odd star go to dance with men in uniform. I had a dance with Gloria Swanson. I only took about a dozen steps before I was cut out but still I can say I danced with her.

Ian also attended a luncheon with Australian Broadway actress Lady Suzanne Wilkins, wife of the polar explorer Sir Hubert Wilkins. (She had once complained that she had seen her husband for only three months in seven years and noted that she might accompany him on his next trip as a cook. It would only be a business of opening cans, she said, but she would do that with style.) Another night Ian had dinner at the Museum of Modern Art before catching a train to Harlem. There he took a cab from the station and told the driver to put them out in one of the toughest parts:

> What a contrast to the brilliantly lighted Broadway. The houses seemed terribly overcrowded and the streets were filthy.

The following day he went to Chinatown and down in the Bowery district he met a chap who had been to Australia and jumped ship in Sydney. He was slightly under the weather and offered to show them the real Bowery:

> We let him show us where all the Boweryites slept and got drunk. We went to a beer dive where beer and liquors could be obtained for ten cents a shot. And supposedly could knock you rotten. The chap we were with kept telling us if we got into a fight he wasn't having anything

to do with us. But the first thing he did was tip another man's beer on the floor and cop a wallop in the snout for it. We stayed in the place for about ten minutes just watching how these dregs of humanity behave.

In between social observation, Ian took a quick tour of the Statue of Liberty and LaGuardia Airport. He had hoped to catch up with the Krafts but was informed that none was currently in New York. As a consolation to his father he added, 'I bought some Kraft caramels'.

When Ian's American gallivant was over, he made his way by train back across the border to an embarkation depot in Halifax, Nova Scotia. There he joined his fellow airmen to play the waiting game. He wrote that the main street was very shabby and little better than 'the poorest parts of Collingwood':

> Halifax has about two men in uniform to every civilian, as there are hundreds of sailors, soldiers and airmen. There are lots of people either blind, crippled or with scars on their faces as a result of the big explosion in 1917 when a ship loaded with TNT exploded after catching fire.

The 1917 disaster was the biggest man-made explosion in history at that time. Some reports had debris from the harbour landing eight kilometres away.

By now Ian had nearly fifty hours' flying under his belt and had also undertaken his first solo night flight. He was delighted to announce to his father that he had gained his wings, despite the fact that he couldn't have flown any worse during the final flying test.

In a letter dated Anzac Day 1942 I discovered that my father Bill had joined the RAAF and was then at a training camp learning Morse code. Ian told my father that a remembrance ceremony had been held that morning in Halifax and that about twelve hundred Australian and New Zealand airmen were in attendance:

> We observed 2 minutes silence and placed a couple of wreaths in memory of the fallen. We have the afternoon off and will probably have a game of Australian Rules football.

He signed off with a parting shot at his little brother's sporting prowess.

> I haven't had a game [of tennis] since I left home, although I have lugged my racket halfway around the world. However I don't think you need to get too cocky and think I still can't wipe you off the court.

Finally Ian's wait was over. He boarded the MS *Batory*, a former Polish cruise ship, bound for England. Unlike the young pilot, the vessel had already had an active war, spiriting away thousands of troops in the evacuation of Dunkirk and secretly transporting more than £40 million worth of the English gold reserve from Scotland to Canada.

For Ian there was only excitement. He told his father that he would now have 'a chance to fly a real thoroughbred'.

Fighting Men, Fighting Fit

An advertisement for Vegemite from the early 1940s includes an artist's impression of a man resembling my grandfather and two airforce pilots. The headline, 'Someone must be getting all the Vegemite', played upon the scarcity that was finally making, through absence, Australian hearts grow fonder.

The copy went on to tell how Cyril's vitamin-packed spread was helping to lead the injured back to useful civilian life and keeping 'fighting men fighting fit'. What was more, the supplies that stayed on Australian soil were required to protect the young and frail. Gratuitous consumption by other civilians would have caused a moral outrage:

You wouldn't deny that children, babies and invalids should have first claim on Vegemite – would you? Of course not … Vegemite is exactly what they need.

Another advertisement played on a young slouch-hatted boy's love for his absent father.

Young Peter loves Vegemite … and his mother loves giving it to him … but he's not getting so much these days, as his mother says, 'It's nearly all going to Daddy, darling.' And she's right! The Vegemite is needed for our fighting men.

The public was now forced to tolerate the shortage of a foodstuff that Kraft Walker could barely give away a few years earlier.

Wartime austerity meant a newfound thrift and resourcefulness. People began recycling and conserving and growing their own vegetables. The priority at all times was to package food in bulk for the armed forces and the needs of civilians came second.

As mobilisation intensified, Kraft's output rose over one hundred per cent and the company's US newsletter, *Kraftsman*, declared the Melbourne operation to be the Australian equivalent of Kraft's Chicago headquarters. Production could only keep pace with demand by the recruitment of volunteers of all ages.

In Australia almost every man woman and child is engaged in war work but still there are not enough hands to do the tasks. In some of the plants production has been kept up through the efforts of school children, housewives and others who are willing to come in and spend their after school or evening hours lending a helping hand.

The Australian government introduced an hour of daylight saving in summer to help shift workers and reduce fuel wastage in running artificial lighting. One week's paid annual leave was the only rest many had.

Cyril spent his holidays in seaside Lorne on the Great Ocean Road and appeared finally to be making a full recovery, walking to the beach twice a day. It was a feat Ian encouragingly declared 'not bad in the summer heat'.

Ian shared a cabin on his Britain-bound ship with five others, but as there were only four bunks they took turns sleeping on the floor. They were right on the waterline and couldn't open their porthole but, as others had only hammocks on the open deck, no complaints were raised. A fleet of battleships and cruisers escorted them across the Atlantic but Ian knew any further detail he revealed by letter would go the way of the *Monterey* brochure and fall victim to the censor's knife. It didn't take much to read between the lines. Upon reaching Scotland he told his parents that he was prevented from disclosing the exact point of disembarkation, 'suffice to say it's about 90 miles [145 kilometres] from mother's home town'.

The coastline was strewn with fortifications, the harbour full of barrage balloons and the beaches strung with barbed wire. The airmen boarded a train for the border city of Carlisle, only sixteen kilometres from Cyril's old headquarters at Gretna Green. Unlike in those times there were no whiskies lined up waiting on the bar. Every building of significance that they passed was heavily camouflaged and for good reason. One town they stopped at, Bath, had only a week earlier been blitzed for eight hours one night and five the next. The damage was horrific and thirteen hundred people had lost their lives. The men changed trains and headed south to the seaside resort town of Bournemouth.

> I had my first swim since leaving Australia, the beach was quite warm but the water must have come straight from the Pole.

A few days later Ian received a week's leave and took a train to London. He shared a carriage with a cockney couple and their extended family who were returning home after the blitz.

In London he stayed with his mother's sister Rebe, whose home, he reported, had so far escaped damage from the shelling. As in New York, each day was crammed solid with sightseeing. He told his parents that Buckingham Palace didn't seem so impressive surrounded by sandbags and festooned with blackout shutters.

A failed attempt to enter Westminster was followed by a stroll along the Thames embankment where Antarctic explorer Robert Scott's ship, the *Discovery*, was moored. In the ensuing days Ian took in Madame Tussaud's, enjoyed lunch at the Boomerang Club at Australia House and observed that the nearby church of St Clement's had been razed to the ground.

War was also having subtler impacts on many British landmarks. Ian visited London Zoo and the Tower of London only to find that most of the animals had been evacuated and the Crown Jewels relocated for safekeeping. The Beefeaters had turned the moat encircling the Tower into a vegetable garden and Ian mused that it seemed quite the practice to grow crops wherever possible. At Windsor Castle he was shown around by a schoolboy from Eton who had a 'dodgy accent', a jumper that needed mending and shoes that needed cleaning.

Everywhere Ian went there was the reminder that, despite the frivolities, he was no mere tourist. After taking in a show with his aunties in the West End – 'the tickets cost me a pile' – he observed flashes lighting up the sky somewhere out to the east. When he returned to Bournemouth the following day he discovered that it had been bombed.

But Ian's war was yet to begin and more hours were spent in trains than planes. A technical course at Britain's largest RAF base in Wales was followed by a posting to an advanced flying unit at Peterborough in the east of England. He then returned to Grangemouth in Scotland before moving on to an airfield at Balado Bridge near Kinross.

Finally, a July 1942 logbook entry records his first solo flight in a Spitfire: 'The first flip is a bit of a thrill as you are on your own right from the jump.'

He wrote to Cyril that with the throttle fully open the plane would do about three hundred miles per hour. To Jean he revealed a growing impatience: 'Dad thought I would be in action by now. I won't be for some time.'

Scottish weather did its best to keep the pilots grounded, but from the logbooks it appears that on most days the frequent drizzle did not prevent them from getting up in the air. Ian enjoyed the training flights over Edinburgh and the world's second longest bridge spanning the Firth of Forth as well as the cosmopolitan company of his colleagues.

Half the course are Aussies, South Africans and British and the other half are Poles. They are fine fellows and terribly interesting to have a yarn with.

In the evenings Ian returned from the base to his nearby billet with a local family and spent much of his free time chatting, a sport at which he felt he had an distinct advantage through having a Scottish mother. Around this time he sent the family a package which contained nine paintings of Spitfires by a Polish pilot. For many years several of these watercolours hung next to the fossilised fish in my father's study. They now hang on my wall.

A little over a week after Ian went solo in the Spitfire, Cyril wrote to the manager of ABC Radio expressing his appreciation at being notified of a 'Voices from America' broadcast that included Ian's Radio City recording.

By the end of September 1942 Ian had accumulated more than two hundred and fifty hours' flying time. Low flying and formation work had given way almost exclusively to instruction in air firing and dog fighting. A year and a half after joining up, his apprenticeship was finally complete. He was transferred to No. 19 Squadron RAF based at Perranporth in Cornwall, close to Land's End. Ominously, a receipt recorded his allocation of a pilot's chute and an inflatable dinghy. The squadron was dedicated to homeland security, flying air cover over the waters between England and France. As ever, Ian's first impressions seemed more appropriate to a postcard than a letter home from war. There was no talk of the enemy, nor any hint of anxiety,

The ultra-modern Kraft Walker factory across the Yarra River,
commonly known as Riverside, was opened in 1928.

Courtesy of Kraft Foods Australia

Hand-packing chocolates at MacRobertson's, Melbourne, in the 1920s.
State Library of Victoria

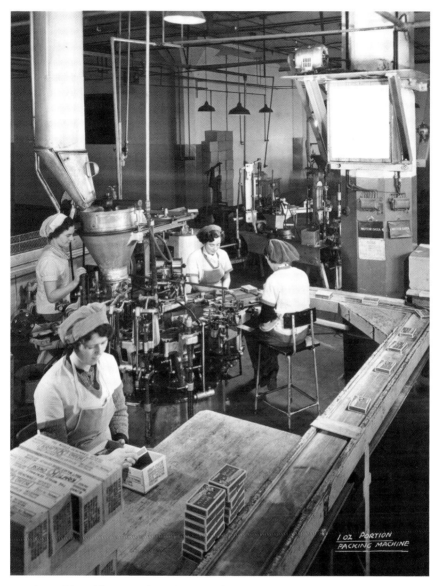

Once Riverside opened, modern production lines at Kraft improved yields
and delivery. Here, Kraft cheese is being packed.
Courtesy of Kraft Foods Australia

At war. The much prized Vegemite ration can,
which saw the paste's popularity skyrocket at last.

Courtesy of Kraft Foods Australia

Some of 79 Squadron, playing cards while waiting for word of action
on Goodenough Island, D'Entrecasteaux Group, Papua New Guinea, 1943.
Ian Callister is the only one looking at the camera. Next to him are
W. J. (Bill) Pickard and W. J. (Bill) Clarke.

P02875.087, William H. Robinson, Australian War Memorial.

B flight pilots of No. 79 (Spitfire) Squadron RAAF near Vivigani airfield, July 1943.

Back row, left to right: Sgt R. W. Bolton; Sgt C. J. Schmitzer;
Flying Officer R. K. Hollow; Pilot Officer O. B. Morgan;
Sgt D. A. Grinlington; FO W. J. Pickard; FO J. R. Richards;
FO A. H. Birch; Sgt I. H. Callister; Flight Sergeant P. F. Turner.

Front row: Sgt G. R. Gilbert; Wing Commander W. S. Arthur
DSO DFC, No. 73 Wing Leader; Squadron Leader A. C. Rawlinson
DFC & Bar, Commanding Officer; Flight Lieutenant M. S. Bott,
Flight Commander; PO W. R. Binning.

P02874_027, William H. Robinson, Australian War Memorial

The wreck of Ian's plane, Spitfire aircraft A58-177 UP-K, November 1943.
PO2875.389 Australian War Memorial

All things modern for bringing new Kraft Walker product to market.
State Library of Victoria

18 July 1945. Kraft employees at the Melbourne plant are
working hard, peeling potatoes before they are sliced and dehydrated,
a relatively new food process at the time.

111137 Australian War Memorial

One of the last photographs of Cyril in his Kew garden.
To this day, no one in the family knows whose hand that is.

just a boy's own adventure in the big blue sky: 'It's a marvellous sight to see both sides of the channel.'

It was to be a short assignment. Ian's Spitfire training now meant that he could help defend his own country from the growing threat to the north. He journeyed home via Canada in the luxury of the *Queen Elizabeth* which, like the *Normandie*, had been refitted into a troopship.

Ian arrived in Melbourne tanned and fit. He visited the Kraft factory and caught up with those friends and colleagues who had remained at home. Three weeks' leave was spent playing tennis and socialising before returning to duty shortly before his twenty-first birthday.

Seventy-nine Squadron RAAF was formed in the foothills of the You Yang ranges, not far from Geelong. It was stationed at Wooloomanata, a property owned by the family of James Fairbairn, former Minister for Air, pioneer World War I pilot and record-setting aviator.

Fairbairn had previously cheated death a few years earlier when, on a whim, he chose to fly his own plane to Canberra; the plane he was originally scheduled to travel in crashed, killing all occupants. Menzies had promoted Fairbairn to Cabinet at the start of the war but only twelve months later he and the Minister for Army were killed in a freak accident. Their Lockheed-Hudson aircraft stalled so close to landing on the Canberra strip that their staffers witnessed the event. Unsubstantiated rumours later circulated that Fairbairn had persuaded the RAAF pilot to allow him to fly the plane. Other passengers included the Minister for Scientific and Industrial Research. Menzies told Parliament the next day that there had been a dreadful calamity:

For my three colleagues were my close and loyal friends. Each of them had a place not only in the Cabinet but in my heart.

The first task for members of Ian's new squadron was to do an 'emu bob' of Esther's paddock, clearing the new runway of rocks and debris. Further training was undertaken at Mildura and Williamtown, near Newcastle. A Spitfire flight over a small country town startled the locals, the Rolls Royce engines roaring as they flew low and fast, tail chasing and shadow shooting.

Finally they returned to Wooloomanata and prepared to depart for an as yet unknown destination. The ground crew left in advance with a field ambulance piled full of food and alcohol in preparation for the 'odd ding night where it was custom to let off steam'. At Laverton air base, south-west of Melbourne, the commanding officer issued the standard parting instructions to his pilots:

> Head north, keep Australia on your left, when you get to the pointy bit look out for New Guinea. Good luck.

Their actual route took them from Laverton to Richmond, Amberley, Townsville, Horn Island, Port Moresby and, finally, Goodenough Island in the D'Entrecasteaux archipelago.

In 1791 the French Rear Admiral Bruni D'Entrecasteaux had been sent by King Louis XVI to search for the lost explorer, La Pérouse, who was last seen departing Botany Bay in 1788. It was said that as the French monarch was approaching the guillotine in 1793, he turned to the priest accompanying him and asked, 'What news of La Pérouse?'

The mountainous Goodenough Island, off the east coast of New Guinea, was named by Captain John Moresby in the 1870s.

In December 1942 it had been the scene of a remarkable deception, whereby a small band of Australian personnel built a series of fake structures, including a hospital, intended to fool the Japanese into believing the island was occupied by a large brigade. Logs were pointed to the sky to mimic anti-aircraft guns and entangled vines strewn along the beaches to emulate barbed wire. The ruse worked and Goodenough Island was transformed into a major staging post for operations against the shipping and airfields of the Japanese stronghold in Rabaul.

Ian's squadron arrived on 19 June 1943, only four days after the island's fighter strip had been completed. The Spitfires of 79 Squadron lacked the range to strike Rabaul, but would provide local air cover. The defence of the island was to be maintained by the Americans on the ground and the Australians in the air.

A member of the ground crew on Goodenough made comment on encountering American troops for the first time:

> We found the GIs to be friendly and generous to a fault, but often very naive. They were weak on geography having little knowledge of the world outside the USA. They were profane to a degree which was almost poetical and made the Aussie soldier look like an amateur when it came to swearing.

By the end of the following month, the GIs were outnumbered, as upwards of three and a half thousand Australian RAAF personnel took up residence on the island. The strategic importance of the base meant that everything was under wraps.

Ian informed his parents that he didn't think he would be able to tell them where he was for some time.

The first night, after arriving late, Ian slept under a tabletop. The vivid white tent pitched the next day was stained with mud and grass for camouflage and, with the promise of a few cans of bully beef, some locals were persuaded to help construct a more permanent structure. Ian joked with his sister that the natives had 'an ideal society where the women or mary's do all the work'.

There were fierce battles raging to the east and west but none within Spitfire range of Goodenough Island. The dust and rain of the tropics played havoc with aircraft engines and the ground crew struggled to keep them operational. Danger came mainly in the form of accidents, as with one hapless flyer who pressed the wrong button in the cockpit and detonated the demolition charge in the radio set.

In the isolation of a small dot in the south-west Pacific, rations became a constant talking point.

> We were very fortunate and lucky people tonight as we had beaut bully beef and cabbage. When I get home on my next leave I'll be very annoyed if we don't have bully for tea and curtin's crunchers (army biscuits) to follow up with. Yesterday we had lamb chops (lord knows where the cook got them from) and tomatoes. Incidentally the tomatoes were Kraft according to the markings on the wooden crate … So far I haven't seen any of Maxam's cheese up here. We always have two or three tins of Kraft on the table, always in good condition.

On occasion their diet was supplemented by other essential items. Ian's mate Louie Turner and another pilot had recently returned from a base near Charters Towers in north Queensland. They were assigned to ferry two Spitfires to the Trobriand Islands off the east coast of New Guinea, and the armourers were flabbergasted when the pilots ordered all ammunition be removed and replaced by twelve-dozen bottles of beer. By all accounts the return flight, conducted at low altitude to maintain the integrity of the cargo, was a success. Only one bottle was slightly damaged and that was drunk by the ground crew immediately upon landing.

In early August 1943, 79 Squadron received orders to move north to the island of Kiriwina, about one hundred and forty-five kilometres closer to the Japanese fortress at Rabaul. Ian set up camp with his mates Dud Grinlington and Louie Turner in a tapioca plantation:

> It took us two solid days to clear a space, build or rather dig a slit trench, put the floor boards over it and then put the tent up.

Kiriwina was a beautiful coral atoll with palm-fringed beaches and golden tropical sunsets, an 'excellent setting for Dorothy Lamour'. But Lamour would have been less than enamoured of the weather and wildlife:

> There are frequent and heavy tropical downpours that bring in the spiders and millipedes that grow quite large

and give everyone the creeps. The millipedes can grow to about eight inches and are big, black, round and fat and ooze a sticky substance that burns the skin.

Conditions at home were, by contrast, bitterly cold. Ian wrote he had seen reports of snow in Melbourne and commented on the recent Federal election:

> We haven't heard the result … but rumours indicate Labor has had a push over. Everyone who was in the Kooyong electorate voted firstly for Bob Menzies. I suppose his local following is still pretty strong to defeat Laurie and co …

Edward Laurie was a school acquaintance who had stood as the Communist Party candidate against Menzies, leaving Ian unimpressed.

As the restless young airmen on Kiriwina awaited their part in the action, recreation was found in playing cards, football, ceaseless banter and other pursuits. Around this time Ian was nicknamed 'Kid' by his many mates. One friend, Louie Turner, wrote that the field hospital was staffed by RAAF nurses who had been given a secluded beach on the northern side of the island where they could swim in privacy. Accordingly, all test flights ended with a low pass over that particular beach where the nurses responded with waves 'dressed only in their birthday suits'. These essential moments of levity made life in a war zone bearable, but they were not to last. Japanese activity was increasing and the skies were fast becoming a more dangerous place to be. On some sorties the P38s limped back from combat while others failed to return at all.

The nips have been showing a bit more interest in the place lately but only at night ... one of the cunning little blighters managed to sneak in without being detected. When the first stick of bombs went off some really fast moving took place. Some chaps hit their trenches still wrapped in their mossie nets, some put their boots on the wrong feet, the boss dived out in bare feet and cut them both (he hopes to get a purple heart for it). I myself executed a movement which carried me from bed into the funk hole under the floor boards without touching them ...

Ian's casual air drew his family's attention away from the injuries sustained in the overnight raid. He described a scene the next morning when the medical personnel were 'trying to load the wounded, who stopped a couple of daisy cutters into a field ambulance and all the relatives were trying to get in the back with them'.

The domestic situation back at home also had its share of difficulties, namely to do with health. Kit, sick with asthma, was scheduled to undergo a serious lung operation and Cyril, although continuing to work, suffered continued ill health and began to develop rheumatism:

I received your letter telling me about mother's trouble ... It's a pity Jean has to give up her job ... Take it easy yourself while things are as they are at present ... I'm in the pink myself and have just had a slice of bread with a liberal amount of 'Marmite' spread on it – and I enjoyed it, although of course not as much as I would have had it been 'Vegemite'. It's the first lot we've had so we might get some Vegi in some day. If I remember rightly you mentioned sending me some … there have been no parcel mails in.

Cyril's response to Ian's letter was predictable. A package soon arrived at Kiriwina. Inside, along with a few textbooks and some antiseptic soap, was a can of Vegemite. Ian may well have been marooned on a war-ravaged tropical isle inhabited by giant poison-oozing millipedes, but his father would not suffer him to endure the indignity of eating an inferior English product.

There were other stories of Vegemite being delivered to soldiers in need. One of the most remarkable came out of Singapore's notorious Changi prisoner-of-war camp. An Australian ambulance driver by the name of Peter Chitty had attempted to smuggle jars of Vegemite to his fellow countrymen starving inside. When the Japanese guard discovered the black goods and challenged him, Chitty responded by telling him that it was shoe polish. The guard insisted he open the jar. Chitty did so, stuck his finger in and began wiping it on his boot. Satisfied, the guard waved him through.

Vegemite and its rival Marmite were actually found to be effective in treating outbreaks of dermatitis, caused by vitamin deficiencies in places such as Changi prison. And in some instances, severely malnourished returned prisoners of war were fed a Vegemite soup until they could manage to digest other foods.

The Kid and the Wolf

Ian swam through the clear waters off Kiriwina, grabbed the object of his pursuit – a tennis ball – and duck-dived, his lily white buttocks rearing up to moon his American assailants. It was a bad mistake: 'When I came to, about half an hour later, I decided against being smart …'

When not flying Ian spent most of his afternoons at the beach, but then, in early October 1943, he was plunged into combat.

He wrote to his father that he 'vectored onto the bogey's track' but there was no interception and no engagement. After tracking empty airstreams for just over an hour he returned to Kiriwina and there had his first mishap.

He brought the Spitfire in hard, collided with a coral bank

and damaged the prop, undercarriage and flaps. The five-metre-tall mounded barricades had been constructed to protect the aircraft from bombing and strafing. It was Ian's first hit, but he dejectedly reported that he had 'swung on landing, the motor had failed to respond and the rudder and brake didn't stop the swing'. The squadron leader told him to forget about it, but it was a blunder for which he was itching to atone.

He didn't need to wait long. On the last day of October there was a special edition No. 79 Squadron newsflash:

> With the utmost pleasure we announce that at approximately 1100 hours today a 'Tony' single engine jap fighter aircraft attempted to sneak in over this island on a bomb dropping expedition … It was seen at 3,000 feet by Sgt Callister (the kid) and F-s Faulks (junior) of 'whatchyer-shelf' fame. They both immediately dropped belly tanks and 'pressed the tit' and set sail after the Tony which went flat out towards New Britain … The commanding officer congratulates the pilots concerned, the ground crew of P and N, and the entire squadron on its first kill.

Ian's plane was faster than his compatriot's, which was still minus propeller tips from an incident a few days earlier. Purple two had encouraged purple one via radio as Ian chased the plane through a tropical downpour out over the sea. A neat ink pen drawing of a Rising Sun in Ian's logbook commemorated his victory. Beside it was written Ian's own version of events:

> Bandit had lead of at least 3 miles [5 kilometres] and superior initial airspeed. After chase of 40 miles [65

kilometres] north from base I fired burst with cannon from half mile range. Observed pieces fly off port wing. Fired second burst with cannon and guns. Bandit blew up and dived into sea.

A fellow pilot recalled Ian's return to base:

As the kid's plane came to a stop he slid back the canopy. I'll never forget the smile on his face or his quiet modesty.

The celebratory 'ding night' was spent drinking everything at hand.

A few days later Dud Grinlington introduced Ian to a visiting Presbyterian minister, Gordon Powell, who attempted to get a first-hand account of Ian's recent conquest. As they chatted they discovered that, remarkably, they had been students at the same school. Afterwards, Ian attended a talk Powell presented of a recent trip to Russia. Shortly after 10 pm, Gordon Powell led the men in prayer for their loved ones at home and the night was brought to a close. Those members of 79 Squadron rostered for the dawn patrol didn't linger.

The squadron leader had already asked Louie Turner if he wouldn't mind Ian leading the way the following morning. The patrol would also provide air support for Wilfred 'Wolf' Arthur from 76 Squadron, a renowned fighter sector commander, who was taking his Kittyhawk up on a bombing mission.

It was still dark when the ground crew connected the lead from the battery jinker to Ian's Spitfire. With a furious pounding of pistons the fighting machine came to life. Ian taxied out, navigation lights blinking until he extinguished them, turned onto the strip and began final preparations for take-off.

Within moments, the duty pilot's light shone green. Wolf Arthur had also registered the signal and urged his Kittyhawk forward from back down the strip.

As his nose wheel lifted, Wolf Arthur was shocked to see the kid's plane impossibly – terribly – close in front of him. He swung violently but the wing clipped the Spitfire's tail and smashed through its canopy.

Ian's dawn patrol colleagues witnessed a searing explosion as the vastly larger Kittyhawk continued to career down the runway. Louie Turner watched on in horror:

> Flames and smoke shot everywhere. The Kitty was about 100 yards down the strip facing the wrong way and a mass of flames. Kid's aircraft was down on the port side with the motor still idling. I raced up to stop the motor. Petrol was pouring from a split high on the fuselage fuel tank, right behind the port exhaust. As I leaned in to stop the motor I realized Kid could not have survived from the mess on the instrument panel. We found him a few minutes later between the wheels of the aircraft.

Somehow Wolf Arthur materialised out of the inferno, his flying suit ablaze. He staggered to the side of the runway and threw himself to ground to roll out the flames in the mud and water.

Gordon Powell recalled the scene:

> Though in great agony he continued to give orders concerning the aircraft and the flight and when the ambu-

lance came he refused to lie on the bunk lest his muddy clothes should dirty the sheets.

Ian's mate Louie Turner gave another eye-witness account of the tragedy:

> We stood at the side of the strip. Me crying my eyes out, until the six .50 machine guns in the Kitty started firing the shells in the breech.
>
> To my dying day, that is one morning I will never forget. Even today I still shed a tear or two over the death of a great mate. An accident that should never have happened.

The tropical climate demanded that Ian be buried the same day. The service was conducted late in the afternoon so that other pilots on duty could attend.

Ian was interred in the allied war cemetery at Kiriwina in a casket of needlewood covered with the Airforce Ensign. Six friends and fellow pilots acted as pallbearers. Powell delivered the eulogy.

> Ian Callister was a great pilot. We remember his calm courage, his gentlemanly bearing and his quiet modesty. He was of a type Australia can ill afford to lose. To me it will always be a memory that I will treasure that less than 24 hours ago I sat beside him at dinner and at 10 pm he joined with us in our devotional service. There he remembered his loved ones in prayer to God. We may hope that that prayer will help them sustain this devastating blow today. At 10 pm he joined with us in the Lord's

prayer to 'our Father which art in heaven'. Eight hours later he had entered the presence of that same Father in heaven … He has died for God his country and for true learning – for culture and civilisation. May God make us all worthy of him!

And with that, all the promise of a young life, of Cyril's golden-haired boy, was reduced to memory.

Back in Australia, the postie leant his red bike against a front fence in Kew and walked up the path to the front door. My Auntie Jean took the telegram.

DR CP CALLISTER

DEEPLY REGRET TO INFORM YOU THAT YOUR SON FLIGHT SERGEANT IAN HOPE CALLISTER HAS LOST HIS LIFE ON THE FIFTH NOVEMBER 1943 AS RESULT OF AIR OPERATIONS STOP THE MINISTER FOR AIR JOINS WITH AIRBOARD IN EXPRESSING PROFOUND SYMPATHY IN YOUR SAD BEREAVEMENT STOP LETTER WILL FOLLOW

The family, in deep distress, began the horrible job of informing friends and relatives. My father, still based in Darwin, had to be tracked down on Cape York Peninsula.

At Kraft, yet another sombre day was suffered as word of The Doc's son's passing got around. My grandfather's natural reserve ensured a brave face, though in private moments of grief he would sit in his study and start a new brown folder, 'Ian's Letters and Press Clippings'.

Cyril's folder contained letters and tributes from Ian's commanding officers and other pilots, newspaper cuttings and even, from January 1944, a transcript from a radio program called 'Spitfires in the Tropics'. The documentary was put together by William Marien, a war correspondent, and it arrived with a letter addressed to Cyril from the Director of Talks, Australian Broadcasting Commission. The program was broadcast at 7.45 pm and ran just on eight minutes. It gave a highly romantic view of the pilots' lot:

> When Mitchell lying on his back on the shore of a wild English coastline saw the conception of his Spitfire in the grace and speed of the seagulls wheeling above him, he could not possibly have visualised his graceful and lethal little aircraft swooping off a coral strip and zooming into warm blue skies impatiently seeking any zeros they might destroy above coral-wreathed seas.

The story mentioned my uncle and others accounting for 'the sons of Nippon'. The Spitfires were likened to 'watchdogs guarding the home paddock'. At the end of the broadcast the listeners would have been relieved to know the enemy was going down like 'quail before the cannon and machine gun' – with no apparent loss of Australian life.

As a young boy my favourite letter in this bulging folder was one that I could not yet read. What caught my eye was the official paper with the strong red cross heading each page. The handwriting was pale blue, the words unhurried and deliberate:

Dear Dr Callister,

It is with much regret that I am putting pen to this paper. But I am sure that you will be thankful to know something of what Ian did and meant to us in this Squadron. The 'Kid' as he was known to all, was quite the most popular lad in the squadron. There never was a dull moment for him and his ready wit cheered us all.

The group leader then provided my grandfather with a brief account of the accident and informed him that there were some photos of the funeral available if he wished to see them.

The letter was passed on to Cyril by Ian's old schoolmate, Dud Grinlington, together with some correspondence between Dud and his wife. Dud visited the Callisters a few weeks later to pay his respects and mentioned that his wife had heard that Wolf Arthur was suffering severe remorse over the incident and was still recovering from his injuries, though he was now being treated in Melbourne.

When Wolf Arthur had been rushed to the rudimentary military hospital on Kiriwina, a saline bath was waiting for him. The nurses were sadly familiar with burns inflicted by high octane aviation fuel. During the Battle of Britain, doctors had found that burn victims exposed to salt water healed better. Arthur required a daily immersion in the solution and his skin was washed until it bled.

Yet after enduring the first session, Arthur refused to let the medical staff touch him. Instead, the task was performed by Ian's former commander, Allan Rawlinson: 'I knew when he was about to bleed, even with his eyes closed. This happened every afternoon.'

In Les McAulay's book on 79 Squadron, *Southern Cross Spitfires*, he recalls the commander's loyal bedside vigil:

> After the bath Rawlinson fed him his evening meal through the bloody gauze hole at his mouth. He would then read the newspaper from front to back – date, price, advertisements and articles – until Arthur was asleep or had enough.

Cyril took it upon himself to track down Wolf Arthur, but he had to wait for the pilot to recover before arranging to see him. Cyril's typed transcript of their meeting is the last document in the brown folder.

Interview with Group Captain Arthur

On Monday August 27th, we met Arthur now a Group Captain, who was staying with his wife at the Lorne Hotel.

He said that the primary cause of the accident on November 5th 1943 was that the signal light from the duty pilot control had too wide a beam. He had complained about it some weeks before and demanded a British light with a parabolic mirror which gives a much narrower beam. It had not been installed and the control tower was situated on the only suitable high ground and had not been moved.

On the morning of November 5th he taxied out of his side road and asked permission to go from the duty pilot. He received this, then saw the light and started off. He did not see Ian until about 20 ft. away when his tail lifted and he could see over the nose and it was then too late.

He said the Spitfires were in the habit of going out on patrol at that time, and Ian seeing the green light took it as his signal, also told the groundstaff men holding his wing tips to let go and started down the strip. We have been told previously that the Spitfires could not communicate with the control station by radio. One thing that Arthur could never understand was that these two men on the ground also failed to see him. Presumably it was too dark. Arthur was badly burned on the back and legs and spent five months in hospital. His face was burned also, but has been wonderfully repaired as he carries no visible sign or scar.

He appeared to be still in a state of some nervous tension as though still unable to relax. His wife is stated to be an Armenian. She also is a very attractive little person. They have been married four years and have one son about 6 months old. They had twins but lost one of them.

He said he had constantly gone back in his mind to the events of that morning as he felt his responsibility, but had been unable to think of anything else he could have done under the circumstances or for the omission of which he could hold himself culpable.

He joined the permanent Air Force two days before the outbreak of war in 1939, straight from school at Goondiwindi near Warwick, Queensland. He proposes to obtain a discharge and embark on a course in Medicine at Melbourne University. It is a hard 7 years programme for a man in his position to look forward to.

He impressed me as one of the finest types of men in the RAAF that I have ever met and I regret that we were unable to have a longer conversation.

It seems typical of Cyril that his words bore no malice or hint of doubt of Arthur's version of events.

Today I am custodian of Ian's logbook, kit bag, flying gloves and of Cyril's folder of clippings. The logbook had voyaged around the world and charted a young man's life. It was retrieved by Cyril, kept by my brother and then passed down to me. I have none of the photos.

Decades after the tragic incident that resulted in Ian's death, I stood in front of a Kittyhawk at the Australian War Memorial in Canberra. I read the accompanying plaque and learned that the pilot of the plane nicknamed 'Polly' was none other than Wing Commander Wilfred 'Wolf' Arthur. Both plane and pilot boasted a distinguished and decorated flying career. Arthur had served in North Africa before being transferred to help defend the Western Pacific, where he flew Polly on numerous successful missions.

In the same year as that dawn collision, Arthur had been awarded a Distinguished Service Order. It was for extreme gallantry in leading his squadron into a vicious dogfight off New Guinea's Milne Bay, despite the fact that his own guns had failed on take-off. Two months later Arthur received the Distinguished Flying Cross for another act of selfless heroism.

At Kraft Walker Cyril pressed ahead with innovative, technological advances as best he could facing the extraordinary conditions imposed by war. Cyril's one-man lab team had, over a twenty-year period, grown to more than forty scientists and researchers. Most were hardworking and thorough, though Keith Farrer remembered sacking a young man for faking results and noted that others did some 'fascinating work, but due to a breakdown in health were forced to resign'.

Supplies of brewer's yeast, that critical ingredient of the now popular Vegemite, were beginning to run short. Kraft had been exploring alternatives to the big brewers as far back as the mid-1930s and now Cyril turned to experimenting with yeast from a molasses distillery, which was, in Farrer's words, 'a by-product of a by-product'. A new factory in Port Melbourne was commissioned expressly for the purpose and a couple of French brothers were employed to operate it. By the time it was complete, the war had been over for two years.

Customised tankers and trailers emblazoned with company logos transported 1200 gallons (5455 litres) of yeast at a time to the Vegemite section of the Riverside Avenue factory. The torrent became so great that workers complained of yeast arriving at 'all odd hours', preventing their participation in the company's social activities. At the Sydney plant, a brewery strike that halted yeast supplies for a week was greeted with relief. But Farrer, like my grandfather before him, continued to explore ways to extract more Vegemite, and more vitamin B1, from his raw materials. Interestingly, he reported that since the war his work had been concerned more with Vegemite than with cheese.

During these years, Cyril had declined persistent offers to take on a high level position in government organising the food industry, citing ill health. I suspect that his lifelong disdain for bureaucracy and time-wasters was also a factor in refusing the role. My father had returned to Melbourne and to working for the old man's firm; indeed, it was noted in the Kraft Walker magazine that he had passed his examination in accountancy.

When the production of immense volumes of ration pack products was no longer required, Kraft returned to a peace-time footing. Yet there were some things that war had changed forever. The once shunned Vegemite was now the company's most popular product and American marketing methods were propelling its rise. The jar was about to sport a young Mickey Mouse and sponsored radio serials were being used for promo-tion. Listeners to *The Life of Mary Livingstone MD* were urged to preserve their own wellbeing by purchasing the healthy breakfast spread. The American arm of the company even reported demand for the product from Australian war brides in its newsletter:

> The husband – a young Lieutenant – of an Australian girl, wrote to Mr. Fred Kraft, Vice-President in charge of Overseas Operations, saying that his wife wanted to find, in the United States, the Kraft-Walker products she used back home in Australia … Mr. Kraft replied: 'You are to be congratulated for having a bride from Australia, who fully appreciates the value of Vegemite and Bonox.'

> 'The Kraftsman' explains to its American readers that Vegemite is a vegetable extract made by Kraft-Walker, and almost a staple item in the pantries of Australia.

In fifteen years Vegemite production had increased thirty-fold and a baby boom would cement its success. In 1948, by way of recognising Cyril's service to the company, James Kraft sent him an American Hamilton gold watch with the inscription 'Presented to Dr Cyril P Callister by Kraft Foods Company in recognition of 25 years of service'. Cyril also received a jade ring and a copy of Kraft's autobiography, *Adventures in Jade*, in which he suggests 'every man needs a hobby'. In my grandfather's case, however, with the exception of the odd game of lacrosse, his career was his hobby. It may also have been his life, too.

The last letter of Cyril's that I possess is addressed to the principal of The Ballarat School of Mines, written on Kraft Walker Cheese Company letterhead and dated March 1949. With it he enclosed a cheque by way of contribution to the school's prize fund and a promise to visit. He would never get the chance.

On 5 October 1949, at the age of fifty-six, Cyril Percy Callister had a fatal heart attack.

Cyril's funeral cortege was led by Robert Menzies, who only two months later would leverage a growing fear of communism to defeat Chifley and return to the country's leadership.

Cyril's hearse made a detour down Wellington Street, Kew, as a mark of respect to my grandmother, who was too sick to attend. It then continued onwards to Box Hill Cemetery.

In the days that followed there was voluminous correspondence extolling Cyril's virtues and thanking him for financial assistance. A few days after that the company car was returned to the factory.

Kit continued to be plagued by ill health and died in the middle of winter six years later, leaving my father and his sister Jean to keep alive the memory of the man who invented Vegemite.

Epilogue

The year after Cyril died the remaining directors sold their private shareholdings to the American parent company Kraft and the merging of firms that had commenced nearly a quarter of a century earlier was complete. The success of the flagship products, the tin-foiled cheese and Cyril's yeast extract, had assured the company's position in Australia. Expansion plans continued.

In August 1950 newspapers reported that a new share issue would finance the construction of three new plants in Victoria, New South Wales and Queensland. The company's annual turnover now exceeded £4 million. The nutritional value of Vegemite would continue to be the mainstay of Kraft marketing campaigns. The important work done by my grandfather, Theo Easton, Keith Farrer and their staff on maximising the product's vitamin content would remain critical to its success for generations to come.

The phrase 'happy little Vegemite' began to appear in print advertising campaigns in 1953 and the now iconic jingle was first played on radio in early 1954. When television was introduced to Australia two years later, a commercial was produced featuring eight children in marching uniforms singing the song. The voiceover strategically urged mums to put Vegemite next to the salt and pepper whenever they set the table. It would continue to air for more than a decade and has been revived in various guises ever since. The fiftieth anniversary of the campaign was marked by a reunion of the children who had appeared in the first commercial.

For me, however, my father, Ian and Jean will forever remain the original Vegemite kids. The image in my mind of them sitting around the breakfast table reluctantly tasting Cyril's early experimental extracts is vivid.

I've also sat at tables and watched people try Vegemite for the first time, egged on by eager friends and accomplices. It's generally an enjoyable show, and it has become a well-worn media stunt to compel visiting celebrities to try the unfamiliar spread on their arrival in the country. A few love it but most can't stand it, and for this we love Vegemite even more.

It's much more than a foodstuff – somehow it represents and defines an Australia that we all feel part of. It is, if you like, an essential ingredient in the cultural glue that binds us together. More jars of Vegemite are sold each year than there are men, women and children in the entire country. But most would struggle to name the man who invented it.

Cyril Callister's tale, like the product itself, had been stored in our family cupboard for a lifetime. My father would occasionally bring it out for an airing, but usually only after prompting by Kraft's marketers to help commemorate some anniversary or other. I remember one appearance by Dad on breakfast television, where he spoke about his father and how proud he was. A title across the bottom of the screen identified him as Dr Callister and we all laughed. Nobody seemed to get it right or seemed to care, and we didn't mind either.

In 1983 my father helped unveil a plaque in a South Melbourne park celebrating Vegemite's sixtieth year. The next day he received a telephone call saying that it had been 'souvenired'. At least someone valued it enough to steal it. On another occasion an acquaintance playing Trivial Pursuit contacted Dad and declared that he had lied to them, that it was in fact Fred Walker who had invented Vegemite and not Cyril. I'd rarely seen my father, a man who had been nicknamed 'happy dappy' by his grand-children, so angry.

As Australia's bicentenary loomed, there was much talk about national identity, reconciliation and recognition for those who had made our country the place it was. The bicentennial committee called for a list of the two hundred least known Australians of all time. I committed part of my grandfather's story to paper for the first time, certain that he was worthy of nomination. It was rejected and my girlfriend, who had only then heard the tale, was annoyed.

My girlfriend later became my wife, and three young children down the track I began to see the significance of Cyril's story as a window onto the times and events that shaped our country. My mother had passed away and my father was getting older. An elusive insight into Australian history was slipping further away.

Shortly before my father died in 2001, I sat with him and asked a thousand questions about Cyril's story but I still wasn't satisfied that I knew it all. The baton had been passed and I was determined to do my best to do justice to the family legacy.

I had witnessed Vegemite become an integral part of Australia's identity, and an icon that grew ever stronger with every public reference and news item. Beyond our shores, it had become an object of intrigue and curiosity, a strangely pervasive national emblem that spectacularly failed to win the hearts and minds of anyone but Australians.

Over thirty jars are sold in this country for every one exported and I have a deep suspicion that the lone export is purchased by an expat.

When Men at Work's 1982 hit song 'Down Under', with its reference to a Vegemite sandwich, went to number one in America the Yanks still didn't get it any more than they had when Cyril had visited in the 1930s or when Ian had received food parcels from home on Goodenough Island during World War II.

When Australia's then foreign minister Kevin Rudd tried to get a jar through customs in September 2011, the authorities attempted to confiscate it and foreign service intervention was required. I suspect it didn't help that US President Barack Obama had earlier that year told Prime Minister Julia Gillard that he thought the stuff was 'horrible'. Gillard retorted that she loved the spread and later jokingly observed that it represented a 'little bit of division' between the two leaders. Past PM John Howard had once observed that more people in Australia knew the lyrics to the Vegemite jingle than the national anthem.

The yeast extract is held in such regard that occasional experiments in varying the product have been publicly met with disdain and controversy. In 2009, when the name iSnack 2.0 was declared the winner of a national competition to brand a variant blended with cream cheese, there was outrage. It even brought my grandfather's name back into the spotlight when the mayor of Pyrenees Shire in Victoria, which includes the townships of Beaufort and Chute where Cyril grew up, suggested that the name 'Beaumite' would be more suitable. The mayor told reporters that he even had plans to erect a big Beaumite jar in the town to commemorate Cyril if his campaign was successful. 'He's invented this product that has become famous around Australia and the world, and it's about time he got some credit.'

I was fortunate to have grown up in peacetime but I clearly remember my friends next door and their grandfather. On Anzac Day he would come over after the march, a brigadier from World War I dressed in the most marvellous uniform, slouch hat and emu plume. To them he was just Pop, but I wanted him to be my grandfather, the man I never knew.

I now feel I know Cyril better – in some ways intimately and yet in others barely at all. He had many admirable qualities and perhaps some not so admirable. Certainly he was a man of his times – taciturn and circumspect. Above all, though, I believe he had integrity – buckets of the stuff. And if I was truly like my grandfather, a man who was fiercely committed to his work and thought about it day and night, you would probably never have heard this story.

New way to treat
NERVOUS DISORDERS

Special, rich supply of Vitamin B₁— the anti-neuritic vitamin.

TEMPER

NERVOUS EXHAUSTION

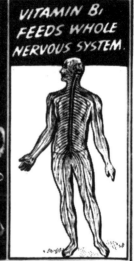

VITAMIN B₁ FEEDS WHOLE NERVOUS SYSTEM.

Unreasonable bursts of temper! This means "sick" nerves. These are usually Nature's warning that you need a greater supply of Vitamin B¹ — the *anti-neuritic* vitamin.

Tears over nothing! If you feel like this, it usually means over-wrought, tired nerves. It means that you aren't getting a proper supply of the vital nerve vitamin B¹.

Vitamin B¹ builds up nervous system. Vitamin B¹, the anti-neuritic vitamin feeds your entire nervous system, builds up those jagged nerves into nerves of steel.

Take 1/3 teaspoonful of Vegemite in a glass of milk two or three times daily.

Do you suffer from ragged, jumpy nerves? Do you get that weak, nervy, run down feeling?

Doctors have discovered that the main cause of most nervous disorders is lack of Vitamin B¹. *Vitamin B¹ is the anti-neuritic vitamin.* Give your system a regular and full supply of this vitamin, and your nervous troubles will soon disappear. Vegemite is specially concentrated to give an *extra* supply of the three vital vitamins, B¹, B² and PP, (the anti-pellagric factor). You see, Vegemite is a highly concentrated extract of Yeast. Doctors and scientists say the yeast plant gives a greater abundance of life and energy. Yeast is the richest known source of the combined Vitamins B¹, B² and P.P., and *Vegemite is a concentrated extract of yeast.* It contains intact all the food elements of the yeast plant in their highest degree of concentration.

Stir a third to half a teaspoonful of Vegemite into a glass of warm milk, drink it down and you'll be taking the best nerve tonic that money can buy.

Make sure that your whole family gets their full quota of Vegemite every day. Vegemite is delicious spread on bread or biscuits, on toast for breakfast or supper, with cheese, with eggs, for sandwich fillings, with salads, and to give a rich flavour to gravies, soups or stews.

IMPORTANT! Adults need one teaspoonful of Vegemite every day. Children ten years and over, one teaspoonful daily, and infants from six months up to the age of ten years, half a teaspoonful daily.

DO YOU SUFFER FROM ANY OF THESE?

✓ JUMPY NERVES
✓ LACK OF APPETITE
✓ DULL TIREDNESS
✓ CONSTIPATION
✓ BAD BREATH
✓ INDIGESTION
✓ LOSS OF WEIGHT
✓ RESTLESSNESS

These symptoms show lack of Vitamin B¹ in your system.

Drink
VEGEMITE
MIXED WITH MILK EVERY DAY!

Sources

1. The Age of Discovery

Dr A. W. Beasley, 'A Pioneer from the Isle of Man', unpublished manuscript, 2004.

Dr K. T. H. Farrer, 'C. P. Callister: A Pioneer of Australian Food Technology', *Food Technology in Australia* vol. 25, 1973, pp. 52–65.

Reginald Callister, 'A History of a Callister Clan', unpublished manuscript, 1971.

Russell Callister, 'The Descendants of William Callister', unpublished manuscript, 2008, 115pp.

Margaret Callister, 'The Bexley New South Wales Callisters', unpublished manuscript, 2006.

William Hugh Callister, notes and interviews, 1997.

Annual Report of Grenville College, 1907 and 1908, Historical Collection, University of Ballarat.

Information regarding Austral Salon and Melbourne Shakespeare Society, *Argus*, 7 December 1909, p. 5.

'Our duty is quite clear…' Australian Prime Minister Joseph Cook, reported in the *Ballarat Courier*, 6 August 1914, p. 4.

'Our last man and our last shilling…' Andrew Fisher MP, *Argus*, 3 August 1914, p. 14.

'Lewis and Whitty's Starch and Soap', *Argus*, 20 June 1885, p. 5; article on Lewis and Whitty, *Argus*, 4 May 1916, p. 9.

2. The Devil's Porridge

Broadmeadows training camp – various articles from the *Argus*: 8 January, 13 January and 19 January, 1915; 1 February and 11 February, 1915.

R. M. Macleod, 'The "Arsenal" in the Strand: Australian Chemists and the British Munitions Effort 1916–1919', Annals of *Science* vol. 46, 1989, pp. 45–67 (Orme Masson quote).

Corporal Ivor Alexander Williams, 'Diary of My Trip Abroad 1915–19', 21st Battalion Australia Imperial Forces, File PR 91/113, Australian War Memorial, Canberra.

Gordon L. Routledge, *Gretna's Secret War: The Great Munitions Factory at Dornock, Eastriggs, Gretna and Longtown*, Bookcase, Carlisle, 1999; 'We lived in hostels…' , Mrs Cooper of Sunderland, p. 273.

Personal correspondence, C. P. Callister to W. H. Callister, 3 February 1917.

A. K. Macdougall, *Australians at War: A Pictorial History*, Five Mile Press, Melbourne, 2007.

Sir Arthur Conan Doyle, 'The Devil's Porridge' in Annan *Observer*, December 1916.

R. C. Callister, Military Cross Citation, Australian War Memorial, Canberra.

Rebecca West, 'The Cordite Makers', *Daily Chronicle*, 6 November 1916, reprinted in *The Young Rebecca: Writings of*

Rebecca West, 1911–1917, Jane Marcus (ed), Virago, London, 1983.

Personal correspondence, C. P. Callister to W. H. Callister, 19 August 1917.

J. Griffin, 'Daniel Mannix' entry in *Australian Dictionary of Biography*, Australian National University, Canberra.

3. Love and War

Personal correspondence, C. P. Callister to W. H. Callister, 12 December 1917.

'When the girl was killed...' Mary Ellen Hind, munitions worker (from document on display at the Devil's Porridge Exhibition, Eastriggs, Annan, Dumfries and Galloway); also from *Gretna's Secret War* and at www.iknow-scotland.co.uk/tourist_information/south_west/grenta_green/womens_roles_munitions.htm.

Lieutenant W. A. Carne, 'In Good Company: An Account of the 6th Machine Gun Company A.I.F. in Search of Peace 1915–19', 6th Machine Gun Company (A.I.F.) Association, Melbourne.

4. Cyril and Fred

Garnet and Sheila Alsop (nee Walker), 'A Family Memoir', unpublished manuscript.

K. T. H. Farrer, 'What Manner of Man', essay on Fred Walker, unpublished manuscript, given to J. Callister by author.

Bonox advertisement, *Mercury,* 10 December 1919, p. 6.

K. T. H. Farrer, *To Feed a Nation: A History of Australian Food Science and Technology*, CSIRO Publishing, Melbourne, 2005.

5. Inventing an Icon

'The Story of Vegemite's Jar and Label', Kraft Foods brochure, 8pp.

Personal correspondence, K. T. H. Farrer to J. I. Callister, 21 June 2009.

Kraft Foods and Margaret Pittaway, *The Big Vegemite Party Book*, Hill of Content Publishing, Melbourne, 1992.

'Lambton Mount. Romantic Career?', *Sydney Morning Herald*, 22 July 1931, p. 8.

6. The Big Cheese

James Lewis Kraft, *Adventures in Jade*, Henry Holt Publishers, New York, 1947.

K. T. H. Farrer, 'What Manner of Man?', ibid.

'American Cheese Company to Operate in Australia', *Argus*, 19 May 1926, p. 26.

Squizzy Taylor: *Truth,* 29 October 1927, p. 7; *Argus*, 28 October 1927, p.15; entry in *Australian Dictionary of Biography* by Chris McConville.

Notes from meeting between J. I. Callister and Rodney Alsop, June 2009.

7. Pioneers, Pigeons and Parwill

Obituary Notice, Robert Henry Aders Plimmer (1877–1955) in *Journal of Biochemistry* vol. 62, 1956, p. 353.

L. Tilley, 'Audrey Cahn: A Nonagenarian Scientist Remembers the Early Days', WISENET Journal number 49, November 1998.

Kraftease pills quote, CheeseKraft, Kraft Walker Company newsletter, April 1931, courtesy of Kraft Foods Australia.

8. The Wider World

'In Yesterday's Courier', *Brisbane Courier*, 10 March 1928, p. 29.

'Devastating Eloquence', *Brisbane Courier*, 13 July 1929, p. 14.

Law Report, *Brisbane Courier*, 18 July 1929, p. 14.

Robert Gotterson QC, 'Hearsay', *Journal of the Queensland Bar Association* issue 55, April 2012.

Wendy Lowenstein, *Weevils in the Flour: An Oral Record of the 1930s Depression in Australia*, Scribe, Melbourne, 1981.

Personal correspondence, C. P. Callister to R. C. Callister, 13 July 1930.

'The Last Moments of a Sinking Liner' in *Popular Mechanics*, November 1930, p. 711.

Steve Brew, *Greycliffe: Stolen Lives*, Navarine Publishing, Woden ACT, 2003.

9. The Doc

C. P. Callister, technical reports. Cyril wrote hundreds of reports after touring other company plants around the world – the UK, Germany, Denmark, Switzerland, USA, Canada are just a few countries he visited – observing and commenting on all manner of techniques. All of these papers belong to the Kraft Foods archive, Kraft Foods Australia, Fishermans Bend, Melbourne.

Personal correspondence, C. P. Callister to Dean of Science, The University of Melbourne, February 1931.

Personal correspondence, Professor Hartung to C. P. Callister, April 1931.

Receipt, University of Melbourne, May 1931.

Kraft Walker Company sales booklet (for staff), 1933, courtesy Kraft Foods Australia.

Dr Allan Beasley, unpublished family memoir, given to the author by his cousin Ian Beasley, 2000.

10. Modern Science

L. Tilley, 'Audrey Cahn ...', ibid.

Transcripts of interviews with W. H. Callister by author and Libby Callister, Brisbane, 1997.

Obituary, Mr Fred Walker, *Argus*, 22 July 1935, p. 8.

Funeral report, Fred Walker, *Argus*, 24 July 1935, p. 6.

Dr C. P. Callister, 'About Ourselves', *KraftNews* vol. 1, July 1945, pp. 4–5, courtesy Kraft Foods Australia.

Personal correspondence, Derek Shew to Bill Callister,
21 October 1998.

Anne Chamberlain and Derek Shew, 'Australian Dairy
Foods', Dairy Industry Association of Australia, Melbourne,
June 2012.

K. T. H. Farrer, 'Reminiscences of Kraft Research and
Development', unpublished manuscript, February 2006,
given to the author, June 2009.

'Appleroth, Adolphus Herbert Frederick Norman (1886–1952)'
entry in *Australian Dictionary of Biography* by Paul Brunton.

Personal correspondence, Robert Sinclair to Bill Callister,
3 October 1998.

Personal correspondence, Bert Gilbert to Bill Callister,
16 November 1998.

11. Boiling Point

Interview, K. T. H. Farrer by J. I. Callister, transcribed by
S. A. Callister, June 2009.

'Everyone Needs Vegemite for Nerves of Steel,' print advertisement, *The Big Vegemite Party Book*, p. 58.

Notes, Bill Callister, 1997.

C. Stanton Hicks, *Who Called the Cook a Bastard?*, Keyline
Publishing, Sydney, 1972.

The Scotch Collegian Magazine, August 1944, Scotch College,
Hawthorn, Victoria.

12. Up in the Air

I. H. Callister, Official certificate of recognition of service, City of Kew, Melbourne, 18 November 1941.

Personal correspondences, I. H. Callister, ibid.

Flight Sergeant I. H. Callister, pilot logbook and service diary.

Typed copy of personal correspondence, Flight Lieutenant Ralph Halkyard to Minnie Callister, June 1944.

13. Fighting Men, Fighting Fit

Vegemite press advertisement circa 1940s, *The Big Vegemite Party Book*, ibid.

'In Australia almost every man woman and child ...,' *Kraftsman* USA November/December 1943.

Personal correspondences, I. H. Callister.

Personal correspondence from C. P. Callister to L. R. Thomas, Manager (Acting), Australian Broadcasting Commission, 24 July 1944.

Menzies quote from the *Argus*, Thursday 15 August 1940, p. 2.

Lex McAulay, *Southern Cross Spitfires 79 Squadron RAAF 1943–45*, Banner Books, 2011.

Danielle Clode, *Voyages to the South Seas*, Miegunyah Press, Melbourne University Publishing, Melbourne, 2008.

Norman Medew, *Up North in Forty Three*, self-published, Sale, Victoria, 1989.

Roland Perry, *The Changi Brownlow*, Hachette, Sydney, 2010, p. 151.

14. The Kid and the Wolf

Personal correspondences, I. H. Callister.

Special edition, no. 79 Interceptor Fighter Squadron Newsflash, 3 October 1943.

I. H. Callister, pilot logbook.

Personal correspondence, Max Bott to Dr C. P. Callister, November 1943.

Gordon Powell, address, *The Scotch Collegian,* August 1944, p. 92.

Louie Turner quotes from *Southern Cross Spitfires*, p. 60.

Personal correspondence, Gordon Powell to Dr C. P. Callister, 6 November 1943.

Telegram to Dr C. P. Callister from the Minister for Air and Airboard RAAF, 6 November 1943.

K. T. H. Farrer, 'Food Technology in Australia', ibid.

I. H. Callister papers and press clippings held by C. P. Callister.

William Marien, 'Spitfires in the Tropics', transcript of radio broadcast, Australian Broadcasting Commission, 13 January 1944.

Personal correspondence, Flight Officer David Hopton to Dr C. P. Callister, 10 November 1943.

Personal correspondences to C. P. Callister, authors unknown.

Reports on events from 31 October 1943 to 5 November 1943, author unknown.

Article, '"Spit" Pilots in the Admiraltys', *Melbourne Herald,* 26 April 1944.

K. T. H. Farrer, 'Fascinating work done but due to ill health … had to resign' from 'Reminiscences of Kraft Research and Development', ibid.

'The husband of a young Lieutenant – of an Australian girl …' from *KraftNews* vol.4, 1946, p. 26.

Personal correspondence from Dr C. P. Callister to the Principal, Ballarat School of Mines, March 1949.

Acknowledgments

This book has been shaped by destiny in so many ways: chance meetings, the discovery of previously unsourced material and other weird and wonderful events. The end result is the culmination of extraordinary circumstance and hard work by a small group of individuals. And they have helped make this a delightfully rich and rewarding journey for me.

Firstly to my wife Libby for her unshakeable belief in the project from the very beginning – a long time ago – I say thank you from the bottom of my heart. I also thank her for putting food on the table, even if I had to cook it! To my children – Sophie for helping with research and reading anything that was put in front of her, and Nick and Lucy for their patience and understanding when all they wanted to do was go surfing.

To my publisher Melanie Ostell for her vision, tenacity and hard work in making this project a reality. At all times she demanded scholarship and excellence and set the bar at times what seemed impossibly high. Often I felt she had been sent by my late grandfather to keep an eye on me. She also introduced me to Rod Howard. This book wouldn't be what it is without his tremendous efforts. He brought a wealth of research to this project and gave it depth and balance, in addition to being a wonderful mentor and becoming a friend. Any mistakes or inaccuracies are mine and mine alone.

I will always be indebted to my grandfather's friend and colleague Keith Farrer, who sadly passed away the same week the manuscript was completed. He provided a detailed body of work, both published and unpublished, and I enjoyed many rewarding conversations with him. He was the last link with a lost generation and provided a wonderful insight and connection with the past.

I owe a debt of gratitude to other family members, particularly Russell and Rita Callister for their work on the original Callister clan. Thanks also to Margaret Callister for her lucid memoirs and engaging conversation, and to Lynette and Ian Ament. My cousin Dr Ian Beasley and his wife Kristine deserve special thanks – I will miss our many inspiring Friday phone conversations. Kristine's brother, Russell Guest, was also a great help in passing on valuable military information. Anne and Rob Lowe provided material for the book and Anne gave me a wonderful insight into the life of my Auntie Jean, her mother.

To my youngest sister Debbie for her delight in the joint discovery of our unknown past and in memory of our dear sister Mandy. To my older brothers – Warwick and Gavin – and sister Julia, and all their partners, thanks for a lifetime of support. James Fleming helped with specific aspects of chemistry and Prue Wales provided sage advice in the early stages.

People who agreed there was a superb story to tell before I began writing include Frank Wilkie, Mick and Jacqui Winmill and the extended Cohen family. Also my wife's parents, Geoff and especially Margaret Cohen, for her help as deadlines loomed among the chaos of family and teenage life.

A special thankyou to Rodney Alsop for telling me about his grandfather Fred Walker. I'd also like to thank Langdon Badger and Lex McAulay for further advice, Anne Chamberlain for information on the Australian dairy industry, and staff at the University of Melbourne and Ballarat libraries, Temora Aviation Museum and the Australian War Memorial, Canberra. A special thankyou to Bruce Smith, archivist at Kraft and to Simon Talbot for allowing access to the fantastic Kraft photos at the eleventh hour. To my fellow writers and staff at the River Read thank you for all the good times and laughter. Many thanks to my old friends and in particular the irrepressible Effie for suggesting I speak to Melanie. To those people I have missed, sorry and thank you.

Index